Market Yourself for Success

Richard A. Payne, author of *How to Get a Better Job Quicker*, is the chairman and founder of Payne-Lendman Inc., one of the three largest outplacement firms in the U.S., which has helped more than 5,000 career persons pursue new job opportunities in the past two years. He has taught search strategy and career management courses at New York University and for fourteen years was directly involved in packaged goods advertising and marketing. Payne is included in *Who's Who in the East* and *Current American Authors*. He is an honors graduate of both Princeton and the Harvard Business School.

RICHARD A. PAYNE

Market Yourself for Success

A SPECTRUM BOOK

Prentice-Hall, Inc., Englewood Cliffs, New Jersey 07632

Library of Congress Cataloging in Publication Data

Payne, Richard A.
  Market yourself for success.

  "A Spectrum Book"
  Includes index.
  1. Success.   2. Vocational guidance.   I. Title.
HF5386.P385 1983   650.1'4   83-21131
ISBN 0-13-558099-4
ISBN 0-13-558081-1 (pbk.)

ISBN 0-13-558099-4

ISBN 0-13-558081-1 {PBK.}

Editorial/production supervision by Louise M. Marcewicz
Manufacturing buyer: Patrick Mahoney

This book is available at a special discount when ordered
in bulk quantities. Contact Prentice-Hall, Inc., General
Publishing Division, Special Sales, Englewood Cliffs, N.J. 07632.

1   2   3   4   5   6   7   8   9   10

Printed in the United States of America

Prentice-Hall International, Inc., *London*
Prentice-Hall of Australia Pty. Limited, *Sydney*
Prentice-Hall of Canada Inc., *Toronto*
Prentice-Hall of India Private Limited, *New Delhi*
Prentice-Hall of Japan, Inc., *Tokyo*
Prentice-Hall of Southeast Asia Pte. Ltd., *Singapore*
Whitehall Books Limited, *Wellington, New Zealand*
Editora Prentice-Hall do Brasil Ltda., *Rio de Janeiro*

To Judy, Bryan, Kent, Michael, Doug, and Todd,
the most important people in my life.

Contents

Market Yourself for Success

Introduction

Even though we've never met, I know something about you. The fact that you opened this book tells me you're interested in attaining success, and you're at least willing to consider new ways of achieving it. If you are this kind of person, read on. You'll find this book about personal marketing to be fascinating reading.

In its simplest terms, personal marketing involves a single concept: taking the principles of packaged goods marketing and applying them to *you*. What is packaged goods marketing? In a nutshell, it's the highly disciplined process used by companies to create and maintain the market for products such as those you purchase at a supermarket or drugstore. Procter & Gamble, maker of Tide, Crest, and a host of other products, is the granddaddy of packaged goods marketing. P&G's by-the-numbers approach to marketing its products is close to a half century old! Believe it or not, many other marketers of health, foods, and beauty aids products climbed on the packaged goods marketing bandwagon more than 30 years ago! The Johnson & Johnson's and Kraft Foods of this world have been honing and refining this marketing process ever since.

To my knowledge, the application of packaged goods marketing principles to individuals like you and me in what I have dubbed "Personal

Marketing" has never been formalized in a comprehensive way until now, although bits and pieces of the techniques have been used by individuals and "outplacement" and "career management" firms. The purpose of this book is to introduce you to the complete packaged goods marketing process and to help you apply each of its principles to your own quest for success. Before you plunge into this book, you no doubt have questions about either packaged goods marketing or personal marketing that you'd like answered *before* you invest your time and energy in learning about its processes. Let's consider several you are probably wondering about.

IS PACKAGED GOODS MARKETING REALLY A SIGNIFICANT FACTOR IN THE SUCCESS OF PRODUCTS ON THE MARKETPLACE?

The answer, an unequivocable, yes! Pampers, for example, was not the first disposable diaper. Chux had been available for years. So when P&G decided to enter the field, its marketing plan was based on creating a product that lived up to the expectations of young mothers better than Chux did. No wonder Pampers, P&G's entry into the disposable diaper field, built a multimillion dollar business in a matter of years. And Crest was not always the number one toothpaste. For years, the minty, breath-freshening Colgate dominated this market. So P&G designed a product with a uniquely new benefit—cavity prevention. Crest, with Fluoristan and clinical evidence to support its anti-decay story, zoomed to a position of dominance. As I suggested earlier, Procter & Gamble isn't the only company to use packaged goods marketing principles to create sales successes. The people at Beecham Products, for example, invaded P&G's turf recently with Aqua-fresh. By positioning this toothpaste as combining the best of Crest and Close-Up (fluoride and gel), Aqua-fresh became the first significant new toothpaste in a quarter century and is now giving Crest a run for its money.

In case you're wondering, packaged goods marketing techniques are applicable to much more than just toothpaste. The list of products using packaged goods marketing techniques is a long one today; P&Gers have infiltrated companies selling everything from banking services to lumber. And, not surprisingly, the biggest success stories in each of these fields can be directly attributed to the skillful use of a half dozen tested and proven marketing principles.

HAS ANY WELL-KNOWN INDIVIDUAL EVER APPLIED THE PRINCIPLES OF PACKAGED GOODS MARKETING SUCCESSFULLY?

You bet. You saw the most obvious application of these techniques in the last Presidential campaign. You probably read how the Democratic and Republican pollsters surveyed the electorate almost weekly to learn about the image which their candidate enjoyed with different elements of the voting population. This research was then used by the campaign marketing professionals to develop specific commercials in order to change or enhance the candidate image in the public's eye; or to decide the amount of time each candidate would spend in any particular state; or to choose the suits and ties each would wear during the TV debates, the politicians each candidate would have himself seen with, the film clips to be shown on TV, the campaign rhetoric and slogans, and so on. All of these things were *clearly* and *carefully* mapped out as part of the candidate's marketing plan. What's more significant is that both candidates in this last election put into practice marketing plans that antedate the current election by a number of years. Carter began his bid for the Presidency when he was still Governor of Georgia; Reagan, when he was in the California Governor's Mansion!

CAN PERSONAL MARKETING ACHIEVE THE SAME IMPACT FOR THE AVERAGE CAREER PERSON THAT IT HAS FOR TOP POLITICAL CANDIDATES?

Quite obviously, neither you nor I are lucky enough to have a small army of research, marketing, advertising, and public relation professionals working full-time to promote our careers. But that doesn't mean that the basic principles of personal marketing can't be put to use by you to achieve all the success that's in you. The biggest difference between you and Reagan and Carter is that you'll have to plan and implement your own personal marketing campaign. But there's no question that the rewards of personal marketing outweigh the effort.

WHAT ARE THE REWARDS
OF PERSONAL MARKETING?
WHAT CAN THE AVERAGE CAREER
PERSON EXPECT FROM IT?

For one thing, personal marketing can help you achieve the full potential within you. All too many talented career people fail to do this. Chances are you know of someone who had great promise that never materialized. Perhaps he or she even complained to you that someone with less talent went further than he or she did, that he or she was in the *wrong* place at the *right* time. Personal marketing is designed to help you be in the *right* place at the *right* time.

Another thing you should know: most career people change jobs periodically because it's the only way they can think of to get ahead. Personal marketing offers a viable alternative to the frustration and hit-or-miss results of job search. By applying the principles of personal marketing, job offers should *come to you* because you are the logical person to be hired for the position you want! And these job offers should come both from within the company you now work for as well as from other companies. Wouldn't it be wonderful if you never had to look for a better job because better jobs came your way? Personal marketing can make this a reality.

Still another thing to note: personal marketing can help you advance further than your peers with similar educational background, talent, and career experience. Do you know someone who achieved greater success than his or her education, talents, and experience would have suggested he or she would have? Was it just that he or she was lucky? Or did this person *seize* opportunities to make his or her own luck? Frequently, successful people *unknowingly* use the principles of personal marketing at some point or points in their careers and it pays off for them. Imagine the impact on your career of *consistent* application of these techniques throughout your lifetime.

WILL THE PERSONAL MARKETING TECHNIQUES IN THIS BOOK HELP ME GET MY NEXT JOB?

They'll probably help. But that's *not* its intent, and quite candidly, there are probably better books that you could read on this subject. *How to Get a Better Job Quicker*, for example, provides step-by-step instruction on the critical techniques of job search. It has sold more than 240,000 copies since I first wrote it. Judging by the mail I receive from people who have read it, it does a darned effective job of teaching you how to write a more powerful resume, how to make interviews pay off in offers and so on.

The goal of personal marketing—and, for that matter, this book—is somewhat different. It's to help you get the most out of your career—to get you the best possible jobs *throughout your lifetime*. In fact, if you apply the rules of personal marketing to your experience and education, you may never need to conduct another job search.

An illustration from packaged goods marketing will, I think, make the difference between *job search* and *personal marketing* more obvious: When the brand manager for Colgate toothpaste or Johnson's Baby Shampoo wants to create a *short-term* increase in sales, he or she decides upon a special quick-and-dirty promotional incentive to hypo sales such as a "10¢ off" coupon or premium on the product. But the real growth of Colgate or any other brand won't come from such promotions! It will come from the systematic execution of a *long-range plan* which includes research into the marketplace and the product's unique benefits; development of a more compelling advertising copy strategy; and creation of a new media plan designed to reach potential new users of the product. What are *you* looking for as you read this book? Your next job? Or more success throughout your lifetime? If it's the latter, read on!

CAN YOU GIVE ME AN EXAMPLE OF HOW PERSONAL MARKETING WORKS TO HELP PEOPLE ACHIEVE GREATER SUCCESS?

Sure, although you must keep in mind that until recently few people applied the principles of packaged goods marketing to their own careers. Therefore, there aren't as many examples now as there will be in years to come. Still, let's consider Robert Jackson, now a vice-president with a major consumer products company.

Bob started his career in the accounting department of another consumer products company. From his vantage point as a junior auditor, Bob Jackson saw that the real action in his particular company was taking place within the marketing group. So he drew up a formal plan to get himself into marketing as the next step in his career. Bob's plan involved three strategies: getting an M.B.A. which Bob knew would qualify him better for a marketing assignment; doing an outstanding job in the auditing department so that he would be seen as a "fair-haired" young man; and, most importantly, getting to know the Vice-President of Marketing better.

After making his plan, Bob enrolled in an M.B.A. program (at night) which he completed in under three years. A few months after starting this graduate program, Bob volunteered to be a part of a special company task force, which brought together members of the marketing and controller's staff and gave Jackson several opportunities to make formal presentations directly to the V.P. of Marketing. Two years later Jackson was still in the auditing department. But by then he was a Senior with a group of junior auditors working for him. Jackson decided the time was right to speak to the V.P. of Marketing about joining the Brand Management Group. Jackson was told "it was unusual but he would be *considered* for the next brand manager's job that opened up." Nearly a year later, Bob Jackson achieved the goal he had set for himself three years earlier. He was transferred to the brand group.

At this time Jackson reassessed his situation and decided that new strategies were necessary to achieve his next goal: a more senior marketing position within four years. In analyzing his competitive position, Jackson realized that his *image* was that of an accountant in the marketing department—a fish out of water, so to speak. He decided a change to another company would probably be necessary in order to change this image that he thought would block his career plan. Rather than entering the job market and conducting a job search as most people would do under the circumstances, Jackson decided on a longer-range strategy for the following three years. He reviewed all the companies in his field and after evaluating growth, products, profit, and track records of the senior marketing people, Jackson determined the half dozen companies he was most interested in joining when he did make a change. Jackson then devised a plan to *expose his talents* to the key people in these specific companies. His strategy to get to know these people involved: (1) social contacts where possible; (2) attendance at industry seminars where these individuals were likely to be present; and (3) development of *joint promotions* involving the products he was managing and products sold by these companies. (You're probably familiar with the "crackers-and-cheese" type of promotions that require proof of purchase from items manufactured by two different firms.) Almost two and a half years after Jackson began to execute his plan, *he* was approached by the V.P. of Marketing of one of the six companies he had cultivated as a brand manager. Jackson was offered a highly visible Group Brand Manager's job. He went on to become the Vice-President of Marketing of this company.

One can only speculate about Bob Jackson's career had he *looked for a job* in the traditional manner as an ambitious junior auditor or again, several years later, as a frustrated brand manager. But two things are obvious: (1) The development and execution of Bob Jackson's *personal marketing plan* saved him the aggravation and hard work of conducting two job searches! (2) It's doubtful that by *switching jobs* each time he felt stymied, Bob Jackson would have achieved any greater success than he did by using the techniques of personal marketing!

At this point you may be pretty well convinced that it couldn't hurt to make the plunge into this book. But there just might be one nagging question in the recesses of your mind that needs to be answered before you do. And that's this: *What qualified you, Rich Payne, to write a book about personal marketing?* A good, legitimate question! I'll try to answer it.

The first thing you should know is that I have had 14 years experience in packaged goods marketing and another dozen in helping people individually to market their talents. When I received my M.B.A. from Harvard, I went directly into the packaged goods advertising business. I worked for J. Walter Thompson, one of the largest advertising agencies, on assignments for American Home Products. Subsequently, I became a brand manager and later group brand manager (at Johnson & Johnson and Cheseborough Ponds). At Cheseborough, I created, developed, and introduced Vaseline Intensive Care Lotion into test market. As you may know, Intensive Care became the number one hand and body lotion, knocking off Jergens which had been the dominant lotion for over 60 years. That success was directly related to a marketing plan in which we positioned Vaseline Intensive Care Lotion differently from any other lotion that had attempted to compete with Jergens prior to that. During my years in brand management, I was a feature writer on this topic for *Advertising Age* and published *The Men Who Manage The Brands You Buy*, a text used in its day by a number of colleges.

My background in personal marketing dates back more than twenty years. When I left J. Walter Thompson, I decided to write a marketing plan for myself. After all, plans worked for products; why not for me? It worked! I got a job at double my salary in six weeks. As you might expect, a number of people came to me for help. I used my packaged goods marketing strategy with them. After that, friends told friends, and my lunch hours and weekends were filled with non-paying clients. I decided to develop a course in personal marketing which I gave (for a fee) on the East and West coasts for a number of years. For the past ten years I've been primarily involved in outplacement. That's the assistance provided to laid-off and terminated employees to help them set career goals and to secure positions that put them on the way to achieving them. Companies such as General Electric, Ford, G.T.E., Lipton, Lincoln National Life, and others retain Payne-Lendman, Inc., my firm, to teach the people they are letting go how to market their talents for the rest of their lives.

Hopefully, my answers to your questions have not only satisfied your curiosity but also intrigued you enough about what personal marketing can do for your own career to want to read on. If you do, I make you one promise: Personal marketing is not only a fascinating way to create your own success, but also, in utilizing it, you will feel a great sense of power. Why? Because you will exercise more control over your future than you ever have in the past. You will guide yourself *systematically* towards better job opportunities and greater professional and personal satisfaction. At the same time as I make you this promise, I offer one word of caution: A once-over-lightly reading of this book is not likely to bring you success. It takes genuine dedication to the principles of personal marketing and consistent application of them to succeed. But if you give it your best effort, personal marketing can help you get the most out of life. And that's a goal worth going after.

chapter one

The secrets of packaged goods success

If you're a do-it-yourselfer, you are only too aware of the frustrating feeling that comes with opening a kit. There in front of you are a thousand parts. You're chomping at the bit to start putting them together. Then you read a message on the very first page of the instruction manual imploring you to hold off doing so! You are urged, instead, to familiarize yourself with the parts before you start putting them together. If you're the impatient type, you may have yielded to your desire to get started and plunged in without taking the time to get acquainted with what you're about to assemble. If you've done just this, chances are you later regretted it. In most instances, assembly is a lot faster if you take the time to get acquainted with the building blocks *before* you start erecting them.

Hopefully the little illustration above will increase your forebearance when you learn that the first chapter of this book on how to use packaged goods marketing principles to make yourself more successful deals with the principles rather than their application to your own career. Experience has shown that you need to understand and believe these principles before you can effectively develop your own plan for success. And so this is the reason for this short delay in your quest for the most life has to offer you.

Seven principles hold for all packaged goods products that make it to the top. Each principle isn't necessarily critical to success in every case. But in total, all of the principles are to some degree *basic* to the marketing of winning products and can be applied to your own personal marketing plan. Let's examine each of them.

1. SUCCESSFUL PRODUCTS PROVIDE USERS WITH A TANGIBLE, MEANINGFUL BENEFIT.

Put another way, successful products *have to do something for the people who are buying them more than once.* In the days before the Food and Drug Administration and the Federal Trade Commission, entrepreneurs promoted pills, elixirs, and salves with promises that ranged from restored youth and beauty to the elimination of every ache and pain known to mankind. No doubt these snake oils of the last half of the 19th century were purchased by many believing buyers. But you won't find many of yesterday's "Atwoods Bitters" around today. And the reason is simple: buyers aren't stupid. If your product doesn't *deliver* something worthwhile, people won't *keep on* buying it. Conversely, if your product delivers a benefit, it is likely to build and hold a loyal following—which is probably why both Vaseline Petroleum jelly and Vicks Vaporub managed to reach their 100th birthdays. Both have stood the test of time.

If you wonder whether this principle affects 20th century packaged goods products, consider this example: About twenty-five years ago, a major U.S. pharmaceutical firm introduced a diet drink that provided a precise number of calories. It could be used in a program to lose weight. It tasted good. It could be conveniently substituted for breakfast, lunch, or dinner. This product took off like a shot and became a multimillion dollar business. But it ended up being a flash in the pan. Three years after its introduction, the product was virtually nonexistent, and the manufacturer was a lot wiser than when the product first was launched. What happened? This product didn't really help people *lose weight.* So they soon gave up purchasing it. A meaningful, tangible benefit is critical to the success of virtually every packaged goods product. There are two corollaries to this first principle that are worth noting:

Corollary 1A: *If you can offer users more than one benefit, your product is likely to do better in the marketplace than competition that offers only one.*

As alluded to in the introduction, Aqua-fresh is one of the most successful new toothpaste entries to come along in years. Its success is traced in large measure to the fact that it offers potential buyers two benefits in a single package: "the cavity preventing power of the leading toothpaste *plus* the breath-freshening ability of the leading gel." If you've used Aqua-fresh, you know that in a single tube you'll actually find both opaque paste and transparent gel. It's easy to understand why it has been a smashing success. *Dual benefits* have been a primary element in the success of hundreds of leading brands in as many different product categories.

Dial Soap used this ploy a number of years ago when it entered the soap market. Dial offered the benefits of a deodorant plus the cleansing power of soap. Downy Fabric Softener offered not only the promise of making clothes softer and static-free but also the promise of making them smell like they were dried on the line. Comtrex, the biggest cold remedy success in recent years, went one step further. Its promise of *multi-symptom relief* in a single tablet provided potential buyers with an almost irresistible incentive, and so it zoomed into prominence in a market accustomed to single-symptom relief products.

Corrollary 1B: *If you sell a product that provides the same benefits as the competition but without the drawbacks associated with the competition, your chances for success are very much enhanced.*

Today Tylenol outsells every aspirin-based product. Anacin, Bayer, and Bufferin all succumbed to Tylenol because it offers the headache and pain relief benefits of aspirin without the stomach upset often associated with aspirin. Bounce is the leading fabric softener for the same reason: it employs an impregnated nonwoven fabric to soften clothes in the dryer. Thus, it offers users the promise of fabric softening without the nuisance of having to sit around waiting for the rinse cycle in order to pour in liquid fabric softener. In a word, in packaged goods marketing, if you can go one better than your competition, your chances for success are also one better.

2. THE MORE PEOPLE BELIEVE IN YOUR PRODUCT'S ABILITY TO DELIVER THE BENEFIT YOU CLAIM FOR IT, THE GREATER THE CHANCE IT HAS OF BECOMING A LONG-TERM SALES SUCCESS.

Based on the first principle we looked at, you might conclude that if someone introduced a product that does a better job of providing a benefit than others on the market, that product would eventually be more successful at the cash register. Sounds logical enough! But many packaged goods marketers have learned the hard way that this just isn't the case.

To be successful, not only must your product deliver a benefit, but also buyers (both new ones and repeat ones) must have *faith* in your product's ability to deliver it. Consider this example: In the late 1950's, Johnson & Johnson, the giant pharmaceutical firm, managed to secure the sole U.S. rights to a bacteria fighter developed by an English pharmaceutical firm. It was an outstanding germ killer and J&J had big plans for it. This antibacterial was dubbed Dequalinium and thousands of hours of research and development was spent formulating a mouthwash with Dequalinium as its active ingredient. Laboratory tests followed that proved the new mouthwash, dubbed Micrin, was substantially more effective in destroying oral bacteria than Listerine, the leading brand. Thereafter, J&J literally sunk $50,000,000 into promoting and advertising Micrin in an effort to secure a dominant sales position in the mouthwash market. Sad to say, the effort was in vain. The major cause of Micrin's demise was simply that it didn't *taste* like it was killing germs! Listerine, which in lab tests was shown to be an effective bacteria killer, gave users the sensation of using medicine. Micrin (the more effective bacteria killer in the lab) seemed too pleasant to be really effective. And its wishy-washy blue color reinforced the mild and not-too-effective image created by its almost bland taste.

Micrin's demise is by no means the only instance where faith in a product's ability to deliver on its claim affected its success. For example, I was once told by a former P&G executive about a problem this company faced when it reformulated a powdered laundry detergent. According to the executive, P&G's laboratory came up with a new formula with phosphorescents in it. This new ingredient made clothes look a tad brighter after washing. The problem was that in the box the original and reformulated products looked absolutely identical. This worried some P&G marketing people. They were afraid that if users of the detergent couldn't perceive any difference between old and new formulas, they'd be unlikely to believe that the new formula had the potential for delivering a whiter wash.

So they conducted a consumer study in which users of the original detergent were asked to test boxes of the reformulated product. As these marketing people suspected, most people in the test didn't notice any difference in performance! According to the story, the P&G people then took a very small portion of the reformulated detergent granules and dyed them dark blue-green. These dark blue-green granules were then mixed with the white ones. At this point a second consumer study was done. This time most of the users of the reformulated product thought it was superior to the original detergent! Why? Because the few dark blue-green granules in the revised formula made it appear different from the original powder! Once the hurdle of belief in the product's ability to deliver was overcome, these users were actually on the lookout for ways in which the new formula was better. And they found them! There's a corrollary to this second principle that's also worth noting.

Corrollary 2A: *The way products are packaged can have a big impact on the level of faith buyers have in them.*

Listerine, for example, made this discovery the hard way. As you may recall, for years and years the Listerine bottle was packaged in drab green paper wrap with black writing on it. The Listerine bottle itself was as aesthetically unappealing as the wrap that surrounded it. It came in a bottle that might have been used for vinegar and was adorned with a medicinal black and white label.

Well, a few years ago an enterprising marketer at Warner Lambert, the maker of Listerine, got to worrying about this drab, harsh package. He thought Listerine could compete more successfully if it were packaged more attractively. And so a decanter-shaped vessel was designed for Listerine, which was topped by a beautiful tapered black cap. This decanter bottle was introduced with great flourish. Whoosh, Listerine sales plummeted! Fortunately, Warner Lambert management had the common sense to stop production of the new bottle within a few months of its introduction and to return to the unappealing bottle and wrapper used in the past. *Why did Warner Lambert management walk away from an investment of millions of dollars in the new glass and plastic molds?* Because the buyers of Listerine convinced them in short order that Listerine's no-nonsense package was an important ingredient in its success —it increased buyers' faith in Listerine's ability to kill germs.

There are a great many examples of the impact of packaging on buyer faith. They range from Janitor in a Drum which uses the powerful image of commercial cleansers to support its extra-strength promise to Oil of Olay which supports its promise of restoring youthful skin with a package that has a sphynx-like, mysterious quality. Summing up, in today's highly competitive marketplace, providing buyers with a benefit may not, by itself, be sufficient to make a packaged goods brand a success. The brand manager may also need to work at creating faith among prospective and repeat buyers that it has the capability of delivering this benefit. As such, both the product's form and package can affect the level of faith buyers have in it.

3. THE MORE MARKET SEGMENTS YOU CAN SELL YOUR PRODUCT IN, THE GREATER YOUR VOLUME POTENTIAL.

A number of years ago I was personally involved in a marketing situation that illustrates just how important it is to reach all potential segments of the market for your product. At the time Vaseline petroleum jelly tonnage sales were on the decline. Our consumer research showed why. Many former buyers of Vaseline who used it for their babies had allegiance to newer products like Desitin. On a field trip to supermarkets, I realized that Vaseline's placement in the store was making this situation worse. Vaseline was almost always on the shelf next to ointments and first-aid products, almost never in the baby section next to Desitin. In response to this problem, I led a task force which developed a special "baby" jar of Vaseline. It looked like a child's building block with colorful nursery rhymes decorating it on all sides. We sold this package to supermarkets and drug outlets as a specialty item for baby sections only. Once distribution was secured in *both* adult and infant sections, Vaseline petroleum jelly's total sales began to climb for the first time in about five years!

Sure deodorant provides another good example of this marketing principle at work. When Sure was first introduced, it was available only in spray form. In fact, Sure's advertising strategy attacked the wet feeling associated with creams, roll-ons, and stick deodorants. Sure promised deodorant users an antiperspirant formula that "went on drier." This strategy helped Sure create a large niche for itself in the deodorant marketplace. But this strategy had one inherent drawback. Sure could never compete in two of the major segments of the deodorant market; its spray form just didn't appeal to those people who *liked* roll-ons and sticks. So Sure's marketing strategy was changed. Sure advertising began promoting Sure's ability to prevent wetness longer. References to the drier spray formula disappeared completely. As you would expect, in due course, Sure introduced both roll-on and stick versions to sell to these distinct market segments! If you want to reach *every* buyer for your product, you need to consider the special needs of each market segment.

4. IF YOU CAN GET POTENTIAL BUYERS TO TRY YOUR PRODUCT, THERE'S A MUCH GREATER LIKELIHOOD THEY'LL BUY IT.

It costs millions and millions of dollars to send samples of any packaged goods product to people's homes. Nonetheless, the masters of packaged goods success invest in this technique again and again. There are two primary reasons for so doing. First, the P&Gs of this world know many people are reluctant to buy anything new. But if you provide them with a means to try your product at no cost, and they discover its advantages for themselves, they are very likely to buy it the next time they're in the market. As an example, when Comet cleanser was first introduced, sample packets were mailed to virtually every household in America along with instructions to use the sample in one half of your sink and to compare it with the then leading brands—Ajax, Dutch Cleanser, or Bon Ami—in the other half. When people tried Comet this way, the difference in its stain-removing power was as plain as the nose on your face. Comet's rise to number one in its category was all but assured.

The success of Vick's Nyquil Cold Medicine is yet another example of how getting people to try your product pays off. Like Comet, Nyquil's benefits are obvious: it helps you sleep like a baby despite a runny nose, cough, or tight chest. Millions of cold sufferers tried Nyquil simply because a sample package was already *in the house* when a cold struck. At this point, these people would try anything. Not surprisingly, Nyquil quickly became one of the leaders in its field.

The second reason some packaged goods marketers sample products is that they discovered *giving* potential buyers a *free* package can create a *residue of goodwill* that will persuade some of them to *buy* that product later on. Why? These particular buyers have a psychological need to return the favor you did them by giving them an opportunity to try your product! Even if your product is no-worse-nor-better than the competition's, they're inclined to buy yours because you were kind enough to send them a sample. On several occasions I've personally seen this principle lead to sales: in each case our company was trying to decide whether to sample homes with a small foil or plastic pouch containing our product or to use a larger and more costly glass or plastic bottle. The bottles turned out to be far more *cost-effective* sampling devices. At first, our researchers concluded this was because triers had greater opportunity to experience our product's benefits in the larger containers. Interviews with buyers taught them otherwise, however. The bottle samples were actually viewed by many recipients as thoughtful purse or pocket-sized gifts from the manufacturer while the foil packets were thought of only as a sampling device. Some of the bottle recipients had actually bought the product as a way of showing their appreciation! In short, a good-sized sample can create a thankful market for what you are selling.

5. THE MORE AVAILABLE YOUR PRODUCT IS, THE GREATER ITS CHANCES FOR SUCCESS.

Studies have shown that people generally shop at supermarkets that are most convenient to them even if they are aware of other supermarkets with better prices a few blocks further away. Similar studies have shown that people use banks on their side of the street even though they are aware of banks across the street or a few blocks down which offer higher interest or better services! The reason they do so is *convenience.*

Convenience can affect the purchase of packaged goods, too. Buyers may genuinely prefer one brand of paper towel or soap or dog food to all others, but if it's not on the shelf when they go shopping, they'll purchase another less favored brand rather than go to a second supermarket which has it. *Brand loyalty*, as packaged goods marketers call this phenomenon, varies by product category. But in every case, *availability* of your product impacts on total sales. How do successful packaged goods marketers make sure their product is available when you need it? By proliferating the number of sizes and flavors of their product on the theory that the more sizes there are, the more the supermarket stocks, and the less chance that the product will be sold out when you come to buy it.

The next time you're in the toothpaste section, you can see this principle at work. There you'll notice *five sizes* plus *two flavors* plus *two styles* (gel and paste) of Crest toothpaste! This array of packages is hardly necessary to meet the needs of buyers. Yet almost all leading brands utilize this technique because it helps insure potential buyers that they can at least find a size of the brand they are looking for, if not the size they prefer. Availability may not insure that a new brand becomes a success, but it has helped many a successful brand to become even more successful.

6. THE GREATER THE AWARENESS OF YOUR BRAND NAME, THE GREATER YOUR PRODUCT'S CHANCES FOR SALES SUCCESS.

Put another way, the more familiar potential buyers are with your product, the more likely they are to buy it. How many brands of dog food can you name? How many brands of room air fresheners? Lipsticks? Shaving creams? Research has proven that most people can recall three brands fairly quickly in almost any product category. The fourth brand is usually harder to recall, however. The fifth brand, harder still. Successful packaged goods marketers know it is essential that their brand come to mind *immediately* whenever you think of the product category in which they compete. Why? Because brand awareness—that subconscious familiarity with a particular trade name—has an effect on potential buyers' willingness to try products. In a word, familiarity creates *trust*.

You may have experienced the impact of awareness or familiarity in politics. Perhaps you once voted for a particular candidate simply because you had heard of him or her and weren't familiar with other names on the ballot. You may have experienced the impact of awareness or familiarity when you purchased a major appliance. If you selected a Westinghouse or Frigidaire refrigerator, for example, you may have been influenced to do so based in part on your familiarity with these brand names. Both are among the oldest in the business. The fact is that neither brand is made by the company you believed it to be manufactured by! The Westinghouse brand has been made by White for a number of years; recently General Motors sold its Frigidaire brand to another manufacturer. Likewise, it might come as a shock to learn that Motorola Quasar television sets aren't made by Motorola. (A Japanese firm purchased the name several years ago.) Or that Emerson Electric sold its Quiet Cool-Line of air conditioners to McGraw Edison. Still another firm purchased the rights to the Emerson name on portable radios and tape recorders! (These are now made in Hong Kong.)

Brand awareness, familiarity, and recognition are critical in the packaged goods business. Successful packaged goods marketers spend millions and millions of dollars creating awareness for new brands and products, billions more in sustaining this awareness. David Ogilvy (the advertising genius who created the man with the Hathaway patch) once told me that people are exposed to more than 1,000 different advertising messages every single day of their lives on T.V. and radio, in newspapers, on billboards, etc. Is it any wonder that a new product or brand can easily spend $25,000,000 or more in its first year of existence trying to secure recognition of its name among potential buyers?

To an extent, creativity affects your awareness or familiarity with packaged goods brands. Can you recall what brand "tastes good like a cigarette should"? Do you know where you should go because "You deserve a break today"? Can you think of what brand of soft drink that "things go better with"? The brilliant slogans created by advertising copywriters obviously enhance the awareness and purchase of particular brands versus others.

To an extent, too, the strategies of Media Directors impact on your awareness of and familiarity with certain brands versus others. Given the same budget, for example, one media pro may opt for nighttime television, another for daytime TV or saturation radio. Therefore, *more total* people may be reached with one brand's commercials while *fewer* people are reached *more often* with another brand's commercials. The "mix" of media obviously affects how many people know and remember your brand. Sheer weight of advertising dollars affects familiarity, too. It stands to reason that the advertiser who spends $25,000,000 is more likely to reach you more often than the one who spends only $5,000,000. Copy, media, and advertising budget size all have an impact on familiarity. The thing to keep in mind is not *how* awareness is achieved, but that awareness is critical to the success of packaged goods that make it to the top.

7. PRICE IS A LESS IMPORTANT DETERMINANT IN PACKAGED GOODS PURCHASE DECISIONS THAN VALUE RECEIVED BY THE BUYERS.

You want the best deal for your hard-earned money, and you're not alone. Every buyer does. So, at least occasionally, it's a good bet you switch from your regular brand to another which features a cents-off label, sends you a money-saving coupon via the newspaper or by mail, or entices you to switch with a "Free Extra Ounces" package which costs no more than your regular brand in a smaller package.

On the other hand, if the brand you switch to doesn't live up to your performance expectations, you are likely to switch back to your regular brand. Certainly, price is a factor in your purchase decisions. But when it comes to buying packaged goods, shelf price isn't the critical long-term issue. (If it were, those generic brands would have the lion's share of the market in every category in which they compete. In reality, they rarely enjoy a 20 percent share of total sales in any one category.) In packaged goods, what counts with most customers is actual (or perceived) *value for money spent.*

There are countless examples that demonstrate this principle in action. For example, when Contac time-release cold capsules were first introduced, they cost nearly twice as much per hour of relief as regular cold tablets. Yet they zoomed to first place in the colds remedy field because they provided continuous symptomatic relief for 12 hours. To cold sufferers, they were worth the premium price Smith-Kline charged for them. Bounty, the leading paper towel, costs consumers 25% more than some other paper towel brands. But Bounty towels soak up spills faster than these other brands. Campbell's, long the dominant canned soup, costs far more than store brands which imitate Campbell's. But Campbell's soups consistently taste better than the look-alike packages which vary in quality from can to can and so Campbell's continues to hold the lion's share of the canned soup business. In practically every product category you can think of, the leading brands *charge more* but *deliver more* than the also-rans competing with them.

There are cases, to be sure, in which the leading brand is higher-priced and yet doesn't *appear* to offer any more benefits to buyers than less popular, less expensive products. The nail polish category is one such example. Both Revlon and Cutex polishes are attractive, durable products. How does Revlon hold onto its number one share while charging a significantly higher price than Cutex? The answer lies in the second principle of marketing success: belief in the product's ability to deliver. Revlon provides buyers with unseen psychological value that Cutex does not: with confidence that the shades purchased are in vogue, with a feeling that the user is more attractive because she is using a more expensive (prestige) brand. Obviously these benefits are all in the mind, the result of effective advertising. But whether these benefits can be seen in use is a moot point. The fact is that consumers *perceive* that they are receiving special benefits in using Revlon polish and willingly pay more for it. Revlon is the leader because, for buyers, there's a sufficient value in their perception of Revlon to make it worth the higher price.

In sum, the strategy of most successful packaged goods marketers such as P&G, Colgate, and J&J is to compete on the basis of value rather than price. In fact, these marketers consciously avoid entering product categories where they are unable to create products which offer buyers more benefits than the competition!

There you have it: the seven marketing principles which have spelled the difference between those packaged goods brands that made it to number one and those that were also-rans. As promised, the balance of this book puts these principles to use to help you both plan and execute your own personal marketing success.

GET INVOLVED!

1. Think of a successful packaged goods product that you are personally familiar with. Read over each of the seven secrets of packaged goods success, asking yourself whether the item you thought of made or makes use of each principle (e.g., does it offer a real or psychological benefit? What is it? Does its image enhance that benefit? How? And so on). How many of the seven secrets worked together to help the successful brand you thought of to become successful? If you can't think of one successful brand which used all seven, can you think of different brands you are personally familiar with that used one or more of the principles?

2. Try to think of a *non*-packaged goods marketing success that you are personally familiar with. After all, as suggested in the Introduction, today packaged goods principles are applied in many other industries. Try to come up with your own example such as the Mustang car or the Atari home television game. Then check through the list of seven principles basic to packaged goods success. How many of these same ideas worked outside of the packaged goods field to make the item or service you thought of a marketing success?

3. Try to think of a packaged goods product (or non-packaged goods item or service, for that matter) which was an *absolute failure*. You might consider CUE, the fluoride toothpaste introduced six months after Crest, or the Edsel car. Run through the seven secrets of packaged goods success one more time and ask yourself which principles, if any, the manufacturer *didn't* have going for him. Knowing these seven secrets, what advice might you have given the manufacturer before this product was launched that could, perhaps, have made the item or service more successful?

chapter two

Putting packaged goods principles to work for you

A few years ago the marketing world was all abuzz about a concept called Life Cycle Marketing (LCM, for short). It was written up in business journals; it was talked about by brand managers over coffee and cocktails. The LCM concept isn't at all complicated. Simply stated, it suggests that similarities exist between the stages of human life and the selling life of packaged goods brands. Proponents of the LCM concept felt brand managers should take it into account in developing marketing plans.

The Life Cycle Marketing concept really makes sense. Applying it today, for example, would lead you to conclude that products such as Soft Soap or Carpet Fresh powder carpet deodorant are in the early stages of their brand lives. At this point these products are new kids on the block and require a good deal of advertising support to create awareness of their existence and a lot of trial devices to get people to recognize their benefits.

According to LCM theory, you would probably consider Tylenol headache tablets and Comtrex cold capsules as today's young adults. These maturing products are riding a crest of sales popularity. They are strong enough brands to spawn significant line extensions of their own (CoTylenol cold medicine and capsules; Comtrex Liquid cold medicine which competes head-on with Nyquil.)

Applying the LCM concept still further would lead you to classify Crest toothpaste as middle-aged. Crest's selling powers are slightly on the wane. It is being attacked by newer brands like Close-Up, Aim and Aquafresh. Crest's mid-life strategy has been to modernize itself much like the middle-aged person who tries to look younger by purchasing a more youthful wardrobe or dyeing gray hair. Applying the Life Cycle Marketing concept makes it easy to understand why the people at Procter & Gamble introduced a gel version of Crest and came up with a new and improved active ingredient, Floristat, which replaced Fluoristan.

Taking the LCM concept just one step further might lead you to classify Phillips' Milk of Magnesia or Vaseline Hair Tonic as brands in their waning years. At this stage in their selling lives, about all you can do is keep brands like these on the store shelves as long as possible so that they are available to long-time, loyal buyers. These brands are too old to continue to invest heavily in; they are in irreversible marketing decline.

The aptness of the Life Cycle Marketing concept not only fascinated me when I first learned of it, but it also actually led to this book. If the stages of human life relate so directly to the stages of brand or product development, I reasoned, why shouldn't the reverse be true? *Why shouldn't the marketing principles that determine the success of packaged goods apply to the personal development of career people?*

The more I thought about this possibility, the more intriguing it became. But did my theory really work out in real life? To test its validity, I reviewed each of the packaged goods marketing principles discussed in Chapter 1 to see whether it stood up in real life situations involving people rather than brands. To do this, I had to make minor word revisions in the principles to account for the fact that they were being applied to people rather than products. Even with these minor changes, however, these principles held up remarkably well. Let's review them; you'll be convinced!

1. SUCCESSFUL PEOPLE PROVIDE OTHER PEOPLE WITH TANGIBLE, MEANINGFUL BENEFITS.

There can be no doubt in your mind that most entrepreneurs who make it big do so by providing benefits to other people and/or organizations. The people who dream up new products and services to make life more pleasant for the rest of us are far more likely to become multimillionaires. Certainly Alexander Graham Bell, Thomas Edison, and George Westinghouse earned their fortunes this way in the late 19th century. And, not surprisingly, those who provided benefits in the 20th century also did well. Consider Ray Krock, the founder of McDonalds; Thomas Watson, the chairman of IBM and an early believer in the "computing" concept; and DeWitt Wallace, the person who wanted to read condensed articles and so founded the Readers Digest magazine. The list goes on and on: Edward Land, the man who invented the Polaroid camera; Nolan Bushnell, the person who invented "Pong" (the first video game) and who founded Atari; Steven Jobs, the person who decided the time was ripe for personal computers and who helped Steve Wozniak market his desk-top Apple for under one thousand dollars. All became respected, wealthy, and, by all measurements, successful by benefiting others.

But, you may ask, "What about us 'ordinary' career people who spend our adult lives just doing our part in large companies? Does this first marketing principle apply to our success?"

To a large extent, the help wanted display ads in your Sunday paper may convince you that it does. Companies continually seek people who are capable of making their organizations more efficient, more effective. And these companies offer more money and more prestige to career people willing to join them to do just that. Whether you are a systems engineer or a sales manager, an advertising director or an accountant, you have probably come across ads in which companies appealed to you to help them build their sales or cut their costs. And, in return, they promised to advance your career or improve your life-style.

The help wanted ads should convince you, too, that Corrollary 1A is also true; that the more benefits you can offer, the greater your chances of long-term success. Just consider the recruiting ads which say: "Must have an engineering degree *and* five years working experience in production," or "A scientific or engineering degree is essential. *An M.B.A. is a plus.*"

If you, as a career person, can provide a company with experience in several fields or the skills resultant from having earned multiple degrees, you are a more desirable candidate. And because you offer not just one benefit, but more than one, your chances of getting a better job or advancing in your current one are obviously enhanced.

Does Corrollary 1B prove out this easily? Applied to career people, this corollary simply says that *if a person can provide the same benefits as others in a similar capacity, but without the drawbacks associated with the others, his or her chances for success are very much enhanced.* Chances are you can validate this corollary from your own personal experience. Have you ever worked with any people who combined both good and bad qualities? A genius, perhaps, who no one could stand? A person of extraordinary technical skill who had dismal communications ability? A highly intelligent individual with little or no common sense? If you do know such characters, then you know firsthand why others who were smart yet practical generally were the ones who received promotions, raises, and the like while the obvious geniuses were often stymied in their career growth.

At this point you may be just about convinced that Marketing Principle 1 (the Tangible Benefits principle) is critical to your success. But you may still have a moment's hesitation. You may say to yourself that to be valid, a principle has to apply in *every* instance. And you may personally know or have heard of examples where people with both great talent plus great personal qualities did less well in their careers than others with less talent, training, and personal appeal! I certainly do. This apparent inconsistency in the application of the Tangible Benefits principle to career success had me buffaloed for some time. In fact, I was about to abandon the application of packaged goods marketing principles to career people when I was suddenly struck with an idea: suppose these less talented people were delivering hidden benefits that the rest of us were unaware of. If this were the case, it would explain why some obviously talented people didn't always climb more rungs on the ladder of success than the seemingly less talented.

Then one day it hit me! The types of benefits we usually associate with people (e.g., saving company money, adding to sales, engineering a new product) aren't the only types of benefits we associate with packaged goods. There are a host of intangible, inferred benefits that packaged goods bring us such as making us feel sexy or more self-confident. Maybe there is a series of more subtle benefits that career people offer? A little study turned up a number of these hidden benefits and explained the mystery of why skill and talent aren't always directly related to success in business. These special benefits are so important to your personal marketing program that they are dealt with at length later in this book!

2. THE MORE PEOPLE BELIEVE IN YOUR ABILITY TO DELIVER BENEFITS TO THEM, THE GREATER THE CHANCES OF YOUR LONG-TERM SUCCESS.

Unless I miss my guess, you will have little trouble accepting the validity of this second principle (the Benefits Believability principle). You and most other readers will have no trouble in recalling individuals who got ahead in large measure because they *gave the appearance* of being successful in their positions! These people may not have been the quickest, the brightest or, more importantly, the greatest contributors in their jobs. But they sure knew how to play the role inherent in their job title. And, whammo, they were promoted ahead of others who offered more long-term benefits.

As in packaged goods, having the image of a person who is able to deliver benefits to others (clients, bosses, prospects) can actually help you make these benefits possible. Consider the case of one of my outplacement clients whose early career was launched on his image of being able to deliver. What happened was this: Bill, my client, became bald at a very young age—he had only a fringe of hair when he completed college. After graduation, Bill joined one of the largest, most prestigious information processing firms in America as a young sales representative. Bill's boss at the time was ten years older than Bill, brilliant, articulate, and at the same time suffering from a handicap that he was totally unaware of: a babyface surrounded by lots and lots of youthful blond hair. Bill didn't realize his natural physical advantage over his boss until the two of them jointly went together to make a sales call on a company that was a prime prospect. After Bill's boss finished his presentation, one of the senior people in the prospect firm took Bill quietly aside. The senior executive confided in Bill that he was genuinely impressed by the presentation made by the young sales rep accompanying Bill. Still, the client went on, he did not want to make a million dollar decision to purchase a computer system based on just youthful enthusiasm. Before signing on the dotted line, the client insisted on knowing *Bill's* opinion. In this case, Bill's bald head alone had positioned him as the more senior of the two salespeople; the one more capable of delivering experienced judgments!

The importance of *image* has been stressed by almost all consultants who deal with executive success; this book has no exclusivity on the subject. (John Molloy's *Dress For Success*, for example, has sold millions of copies in both the male and female editions and made him a millionaire.) But this book deals with image in a somewhat different context. The focus here is on creating a believable image in conjunction with delivering benefits. This leads to a somewhat different and more expansive interpretation of image than you'll find in *Dress For Success* or other similar source materials on this important topic. And, again, creating benefits believability is so important to your personal marketing program, there are many pages devoted to it in this volume.

3. THE MORE JOB UNIVERSES YOU CONSIDER APPLYING YOUR TALENTS AND EXPERIENCE TO, THE GREATER YOUR PROSPECTS FOR UNCOVERING THE QUICKEST PATH TO SUCCESS.

At the start of your career, the world is your oyster. You may elect to pursue a multitude of directions. As you move on in your career, however, you may come to believe that the number of alternative paths open to you are fairly limited. The engineer, for example, who gains ten years of experience with one aircraft manufacturer is likely to consider the market for his or her talents as the manufacturers of aircraft or components. Traditionally, the more experience career people gain in one field, the more likely they are to feel their path to success is restricted to this field.

Remarkably enough, in outplacing thousands of persons, I've discovered there are far more alternative careers open to mid-career people than they usually choose to consider. Therefore, the third principle in personal marketing (the Job Universes principle) is one of the most underutilized and yet one of the easiest to apply. Consider this example: Bob, a Ph.D. in water chemistry, worked almost 20 years helping to solve water chemistry problems for a major appliance manufacturer until the 1981 slump in appliance sales. Bob's job had involved such things as preventing pollution during the chemical treatment of metals used in making stoves and determining which coatings would prevent rust in the moist environment of air conditioners, and the like. At the time I met Bob, he had limited his job search exclusively to other appliance manufacturing firms, and he was not faring well at all since *all* appliance manufacturers had been caught in the 1981 slump and were cutting back on professional personnel. After talking to Bob, I convinced him that he might be of value in a broad spectrum of other job arenas:

- water purification equipment manufacture.
- bottled drink manufacture because pure water is a factor in taste or quality.
- proprietary and prescription drug manufacture since in this industry even traces of chemical impurities can make a significant difference in quality.
- paint manufacturing companies since coating quality frequently depends on the skillful combining of water, latex, and pigments.
- rust preventative manufacture since firms like Rusty Jones are faced with the problem of developing new and better ways of dealing with rust corrosion just as Bob was in his appliance company job.
- chemical, rubber, and plastics manufacturing companies since these firms confront pollution control problems on a regular basis.

My list of possible job universes did not stop with manufacturing companies. I urged Bob to also consider governmental agencies concerned with water safety and purity. These could be pursued on federal, state, and local levels. I suggested further that Bob consider colleges and universities that offer courses in this highly sophisticated and timely branch of chemistry. (In fact, Bob had actually taught a survey chemistry course at a local community college and enjoyed working with young people. He had not, however, even considered exploring opportunities in academia in view of the tightening market for professors at this time.) I suggested teaching, however, despite the generally unfavorable prospects for professorial jobs, recognizing there is always the chance that someone with Bob's specialized expertise might find one suitable opening even in bad times and that's all he needed! As it turned out, Bob turned up several opportunities in this job arena.

Bob's case is, unfortunately, not unusual. Career people in all fields miss out on exciting and rewarding professional opportunities because they fail to define *all* the job universes which they might pursue. Recognizing that the Job Universes principle is very much underutilized by career people, much of one chapter of *Market Yourself for Success* is devoted to showing you just how you can identify a far broader spectrum of potential buyers of your benefits than you had perhaps imagined existed for them.

In both of the previous illustrations (the mechanical engineer at an aircraft company and the Ph.D. at an appliance firm), the suggestion that they apply the Job Universes principle during their job searches was met enthusiastically and resulted in both individuals advancing their careers. Quite frankly, they were both lucky that they were able to make a transition to new job universes during their job search campaigns. When you wait until you need a job to start looking at alternate markets for your talents, you decrease your chances of making an effective transition. After all, you go looking with little or no reputation in these alternate job universes, and with few, if any, professional acquaintances in these fields to help you make contacts with people within the alternate job universes who may have or know of suitable job openings.

The time to explore alternate job universes is when you aren't looking for a job! Consider how much easier it would have been for Bob to find a position with a plastics or rubber manufacturing company had he developed on-going communications with water chemists in these industries while he was working for the appliance manufacturer. Had Bob developed friends within these industries over the years not only might his job search have been easier and quicker, but it also might very well have been unnecessary. Had Bob developed a reputation with peers in these industries, he might well have had calls from them about job opportunities prior to his losing his job. But the plain and simple fact is that Bob's outstanding expertise in water chemistry was totally unknown outside of his narrow career field.

As a career person, you can take the most advantage of the Job Universes principle if you apply it *before* you need it. In doing this, not only can you look forward to learning how to discover alternate markets for your talents later in this book, but also techniques for building both your reputation and contacts on an ongoing basis within these alternate markets.

4. PERSONS IN HIRING POSITIONS ARE MORE LIKELY TO SELECT YOU TO FILL A JOB VACANCY IF THEY HAVE SEEN YOU IN ACTION AT SOME TIME PRIOR TO THE TIME THAT THE VACANCY OCCURS.

Jim Cogburn, one of the most highly paid persons I've ever outplaced (he earned close to $400,000 a year) shared with me the secrets of his catapulted career. The first was that he purposely took a position with a consulting firm directly after college. In so doing, he was able to sample his talents (his decision-making ability, his organization powers, his ability to persuade, and so on) to high-level managers in firms that might later become prospective employers. As it turned out, a top executive in a leading Wall Street firm saw Jim in action on one of his consulting assignments and asked Jim to become his assistant. Since this occurred at a very early point in Jim's career, his sampling program netted him a ten-year headstart in his quest for the top.

Jim's strategy for sampling his talents is not as rare as you might imagine. I was advised recently by a client that for graduates of Harvard Business School these days, the field of consulting is one of the two most frequently chosen career starting points. And according to my source, it is just for the reason described. Fortunately, you don't have to go to Harvard nor pursue a consulting career in order to sample your talents. There are many ways to do it. Consider these examples.

Pat Mulhaney is now Purchasing Director of a well-known publishing firm. He got his start with this publisher many years ago while he was still a teller at a bank. Now you might be wondering how Pat could sample his talents from behind a cashier's cage. What happened was this: the person who is now V.P. of Manufacturing of the publishing firm and who was at that time an auditor in its accounting department went to pick up the company payroll each week at the bank where Pat worked. Week after week, he was so impressed with Pat's courteous and efficient manner that when the time came for him to pick an assistant, he asked Pat, even though Pat did not have a college degree and the person Pat replaced had one. The rest is history. As the auditor rose in the company, so did Pat. It was as simple as that.

Janet Hobart's use of personal sampling is quite different. Janet was already more than 15 years into a career with the U.S. government when it paid off for her. By way of background, Janet's first job in government was as a guide at an overseas cultural exposition sponsored by the U.S. Information Agency. Later she served as a writer and editor for the Voice of America. Her career path then took her to the Department of Commerce as a promotion writer and then promotion manager for the department's overseas trade show. Then, as luck would have it, one of the companies that exhibited at a trade fair Janet helped to promote was the information services company that a few months later offered her a much coveted job. In this case, a marketing manager in this firm was so impressed with Janet's sensitive handling of the problems facing the exhibitors at an industrial fair she managed that he invited her to apply for a job working for his firm. And despite the fact that Janet had no prior experience in the private sector and no knowledge at all of data processing or computers, she was awarded the job and joined the information services company at a salary that was $10,000 more than she made in her last government assignment.

While these examples of personal sampling are dramatic, they are by no means unique. You may, perhaps, have been exposed to some examples without realizing it. Perhaps you know of someone, for example, who left your company for a better job and then phoned someone you know about an opening in the new outfit that he or she ought to apply for. This sort of thing happens every day. Possibly there is someone in your company who is envied by everyone else because he or she has ridden the coattails of another, more senior person in your organization. In cases like this, it's a good bet that the senior person discovered special qualities in the junior person while he or she first worked for him or her. After that experience, it is only natural that the senior person should choose to retain those qualities by bringing the junior person along each time he or she is promoted. To some jealous peers, it may seem like a case of AKing when, in point of fact, the senior person is urging the junior person to move with him so he can be assured of a subordinate with the qualities—not qualifications—he has thus far enjoyed.

Principle 4, the Personal Sampling principle, can have a dramatic impact on your own career, no matter what level you are at in the organization. To make it work for you, you need to do two things:

- First, you have to make sure that you are sampled by as many key people and potentially key people, both inside and outside your organization, as you can possibly locate, and
- Second, you have to be aware of the special benefits that you can provide for those people who can help bring your career along.

If you do both these things, you have a far better chance of making your personal sampling effort pay off. As you might expect, both of these issues are addressed in depth later in this book.

5. THE MORE CONSISTENT YOU ARE IN PURSUIT OF CAREER OPPORTUNITIES, THE GREATER YOUR CHANCES OF LONG-TERM SUCCESS.

Suppose for a moment that General Foods, the maker of Jell-O, decided for one reason or another to limit production of this product so that it was available in the supermarket for about 90 to 120 days once every three to four years. You'd think they were crazy, wouldn't you? How could they possibly maximize their potential sales if they were off the shelves for about 44 months out of every 48!

Now, if you will, let's focus on the way career people typically pursue career growth; the parallel between their commitment to personal growth and the obviously ludicrous Jell-O illustration is only too telling. The statistics tell us that the typical career person pursues his or her next step up the ladder of success (either inside or outside the present company) in a *committed way* only once in three or four years, and then only for a few short months!

As if this limited approach to career success weren't difficult enough, this ritual is conducted because the career person starts to feel stymied in his or her job. As such, at the time of the search for better opportunities, the career person usually has limited, if any, support in his or her quest for personal growth from immediate superiors. To make matters worse, all too frequently career seekers lose contact during the intervening period with valuable sources of career advancement assistance and so have to hurriedly reestablish links to better opportunities during their once-every-three-or-four-year foray into their future growth. Perhaps the saddest aspect of this typical approach to career development is that since career people are mentally out of the job market 90% of the time, they are probably not exposed to 90% of the career opportunities that could have catapulted them towards long-term success!

At this point, you might well ask: "Are you advocating that people change jobs more frequently than once in three or four years?" Not at all. What I am suggesting, however, is that career people be totally *cognizant* of opportunities to advance their careers on an on-going basis and that they keep open their access to opportunity sources *at all times.* In packaged goods marketing, managers maximize their brand's sales by making sure it is always available to buyers. Career people need to adopt this same frame of reference.

It's not that difficult to do so. One way they can do this is simply by making sure they let *all* appropriate executive recruiters know regularly of their whereabouts, their current status, and their interest in opportunities that just might develop. Of course, there are other imaginative ways open to you to increase your availability to the opportunity of a lifetime. These are explored later in this book.

6. THE MORE POTENTIAL EMPLOYERS WHO ARE AWARE OF YOUR NAME AND YOUR GENERAL BACKGROUND, THE GREATER YOUR CHANCES FOR MOVING UP THE LADDER OF SUCCESS.

This group includes:

- potential employers *inside* your company such as a former boss who is now in another department and potential employers *outside* your company such as an associate who left your outfit and who is now working for a competitive firm.
- potential employers who have worked with you personally at some time and people who have never even met you and who are

familiar with your name only as a result of something said to
them by a friend.

- potential employers who are *within* your own industry and those
  who are in *totally different* industries. It doesn't really matter
  where these potential employers are today, or where they were
  yesterday, as long as they can possibly use your talents in some
  way.

- potential employers who are of the opinion that you walk on
  water and those who think you occasionally wiggle your feet in
  the water.

As long as potential employers *know your name* and are familiar enough
with your background to realize that you probably know where the water
is, they are part of an important roster which may end up advancing your
career!

The key operative words in Principle 6 are *awareness* and *more*. The
larger the group of potential employers who are familiar with your name
and general background, the more this principle will serve you. A couple
of examples will perhaps convince you that, just as in selling packaged
goods, *being known broadly* can make a significant difference to your
chances for advancement.

One dramatic case involves a brilliant stock analyst. More than ten
years ago he was asked to be a panelist on a brand-new television talk show
that was to be aimed at business people. He grabbed at the opportunity
although several of his peers had previously turned it down since the program was taped on Saturdays and/or Sundays, it was seen only on public
T.V., and no pay was involved. Thereafter, this stock analyst faithfully
appeared on the show—at least once a month for over ten years. Over time,
he came to enjoy the semi-celebrity status the program brought him even
though the show involved far more of a commitment than he had bar-
gained for (more than 150 shows in a decade) and brought no financial
rewards of any kind or any special recognition within his own company
(its name was never mentioned on the show). Ultimately the stock analyst
came to realize that the exposure he received on the show did more for
him than provide an ego trip. When a time came that this brilliant stock
analyst found it necessary to relocate with another firm, his phone literally
rang off the hook. It became a question of his picking and choosing his
next employer. He never experienced the frustration so many job seekers
run into as they seek to locate alternatives.

While this stock analyst's case is dramatic, it is by no means singular. Carl Spielvogel, who for many years was President of the Interpublic group of advertising agencies, catapulted into that position from a slot as Advertising Editor of the *New York Times.* In all fairness, Carl had done well in advertising prior to leaving it to join the *Times;* he had already become a V.P. of a middle-sized firm. But Carl's remarkable ascendancy to the top slot at Interpublic, one of the two largest advertising holding companies in the world, had to reflect the thousands and thousands of contacts—both personal and in print—which he made daily as Advertising Editor.

Now you might well be thinking that the two examples you have just read are really far out, that both of these individuals managed to secure extensive media support—something that only a handful of career people enjoy in their careers. You are right! But that doesn't make Principle 6, the Awareness principle, any less valid. While it may not be possible for you to secure as much exposure as that enjoyed by the financial analyst and the advertising executive in these illustrations, you will nonetheless benefit from whatever awareness you are able to generate as a result of your conscious effort to expose your name and general background to as many people as you can who might at some time help you advance your career. As you must now expect, later in this book, we'll explore a number of ways that you can do this. And we'll explore ways not only to get your name known to potential bosses and mentors, but just as important, to *keep* your name known to them.

7. WITHIN REASON, WHAT YOU ARE NOW BEING PAID IS A FAR LESS IMPORTANT FACTOR IN YOUR GETTING HIRED OR PROMOTED THAN WHAT POTENTIAL BOSSES AND MENTORS PERCEIVE IS YOUR VALUE TO THEIR ORGANIZATIONS.

Most companies have a salary range in mind when they begin recruiting to fill a position. But if you were to ask 100 recruiters if their clients hired the candidates with the lowest salary expectation, you're likely to discover that not even ten of them do this. In fact, it's a good bet that most people who are ultimately hired are probably seeking a larger salary than most other candidates! Compensation isn't as important to prospective bosses as perceived immediate and long-term potential value to both the organization and to the person who makes the hiring selection.

Thus, this book devotes only a few pages to how you should price yourself for greater success. Rather, it focuses on how you can better understand and merchandise the immediate benefits you are able to provide bosses, mentors, and prospective employers, and how you can create an image of yourself that suggests you have the potential in you to provide even greater benefits to your organization and boss in future. (Let's face it, if your boss doesn't think you have the potential for growth, you'll never have the opportunity to do so.)

When you think about it, with just minor word modifications, the seven secrets of packaged goods success translate to seven practical secrets of personal marketing, any one of which can help you maximize the potential of your own career. The best thing is that not one of the seven is complicated or beyond your reach. With these seven marketing principles, you now know the essence of what this book is all about. Despite this, it would pay you to read on since the balance of this book deals with the practical application of these principles. And translating theory into practice is really the toughest part of personal marketing.

Before you turn the page to begin the process of applying personal marketing principles to your own career development, however, here is one suggestion: Approach this assignment as a brand manager would. Pretend from here on out that you work for the business management or marketing department of a very large company such as Procter & Gamble or Johnson & Johnson. The only difference is that your company specializes in developing and promoting *people*. Pretend, that as a brand manager, you have been given the task of creating and executing a comprehensive program that will maximize the future potential of a career person who just by coincidence bears the same name as you do. Pretend, too, that you bring to this assignment the same *objectivity* and *zeal* which young brand managers—particularly those with M.B.A.s—are noted for. And finally, pretend that it is "Marketing Plans Time"—that month of the year in which every brand or product manager must develop a written plan outlining the goals, strategies, priorities, programs, and budgets that he or she recommends for the following 12 months in order to ensure the maximum long-term profitability and success for his or her assigned brand.

If you assume this role, this book will do much more to move you ahead than if you just read it casually. To put it bluntly, you'll experience the difference between "knowing what to do" and "doing it." But don't be fearful that this is a mammoth undertaking. No one is asking you to write a personal marketing plan today that will last for your lifetime. Brand managers don't write plans for a decade. Rather they write *doable, realistic, practical* plans for the *coming year* that are consistent with the long-range goals that they believe are reasonable for their brands. And that is all you can be expected to do.

Interestingly enough, if you take the time to develop a comprehensive personal marketing plan for the next 12 months and then carry it out, it's a good bet you'll want to update your plan every year! And that's because you'll *see* your plan working for you, and you'll never want to be without a plan again.

TAKING A CLOSER LOOK

1. Reread each of the personal marketing principles included in this chapter. Then ask yourself: "Do I *consciously* apply each of them on a regular basis?" "Are there any that I apply unconsciously?"

2. Think of several people who you would classify as successful in your own mind. Which of the personal marketing principles do you think are used consciously or unconsciously by these successful people?

3. If you have applied the Benefits principle, *who* were the primary beneficiaries? Did they respond positively to help advance your career?

4. If you answered "No, the beneficiaries did not help advance my career," ask yourself (a) "Were the beneficiaries aware that it was *me* who benefited them?" (b) "Were the benefits I provided expected of me routinely as part of my job, or were they special benefits that I planned and executed for my beneficiaries?"

chapter three

Setting the stage for your personal marketing plan

Were you to get hold of the Marketing Plans for Crest, Johnson's Wax, or Ragu Spaghetti Sauce, you'd discover they have one thing in common: the first chapter of these documents doesn't involve planning at all! Instead, each of these marketing plans—and for that matter, virtually all marketing plans developed for packaged goods products—set the stage for planning. The brand managers whose responsibility it is to write these plans use this first chapter to pull together all the facts they know about the markets their brands compete in. This background section includes everything from dollar sales trends to tonnage sales trends, sales by container size to sales by store type (discount, drug, food), and so on. All these vital statistics and many others serve as the *framework* for later planning.

In developing a personal marketing plan for yourself, you could profitably use the same kind of background information. Before you establish your objectives and strategy for the next year and the next five years you really need to assess the markets for your talents and the competition within each of these marketplaces. Getting this information may involve a little work. Whereas A.C. Nielsen and other market research firms provide reams of information to the Procter & Gamble's of this world concerning distribution, sales, and advertising expenses, you'll need to uncover the data that affects your career on your own. A good deal of this information is, of course, available to you at your local college library or can be obtained from the nearest regional office of the U.S. Department of Labor. And, fortunately, you already know much of the information about the market for your talents! This chapter focuses on the basic information you should get down *before* you develop personal goals or your strategy for achieving them. Let's take a look at the kinds of data you ought to come up with.

WHAT ARE THE INDUSTRIES IN WHICH YOUR PRESENT JOB TITLE IS LIKELY TO BE FOUND?

If you are an accountant, for example, you might feel your position would be found in every industry imaginable. Conversely, if you are a nuclear physicist, you might guess that only one or two industries would have your title or an equivalent one. If you are in the enviable position such that your current job has broad application in hundreds of different types of manufacturing or service companies, write down a dozen or so in which your position is likely to be of greatest importance. If, on the other hand, you are one of those people whose job has an extremely narrow application like an aquatic biologist I worked with include in your list of industries not only those which currently utilize your type of skills and experience, but those which *might* utilize it were they to develop new services or products that are logical extensions of existing lines.

Feel free to "blue sky" these industries in which your existing position might fit as you make a list of potential employment universes for yourself. Don't put unnecessary restrictions on your list at this point.

For example, if you have had 15 years of experience as an actuary in a life insurance company, you might be inclined to think that only life insurance companies would have any interest in you. But, assuming for the moment that your actuarial experience isn't as narrow as it really is, wouldn't there be other industries that could use your skills? Could the funeral industry use an actuary to help forecast its needs for burial plots and caskets? Could the hospital industry use an actuary to help forecast the needs for beds and hospital supplies for the terminally ill? Could the government use an actuary to help forecast the cost of social security payments to widows and widowers? Would there be other options if you considered yourself as a statistician rather than as a life insurance actuary?

In summary, at this point don't concern yourself with your present experience level, salary, years of service, or the narrow "limits" of your particular expertise. Rather, list every conceivable industry in which the position you now hold might be held by someone like you. *Later* you can narrow your focus. But, for now, why box yourself in?

HOW MANY DIFFERENT COMPANIES OR ORGANIZATIONS ARE THERE IN EACH OF THE INDUSTRIES IN WHICH YOUR PRESENT POSITION CAN BE FOUND?

It's really not difficult to find the answer to this question. If you know the name of just one company in each industry, you can easily find out. What you do is look up this company in the white section of the *Dun & Bradstreet Million Dollar Market Directory*. There you will find listed the Standard Industry Classification Code (SIC) for the industry in which this company competes. Once you know the SIC code, turn to the blue section of this same directory. Voila! There you'll discover *all* the companies D&B knows of operating in this industry! In an hour or so you ought to be able to determine a rough number of U.S. organizations in any industry in which your present position exists.

After looking at D&B's directory, you might want to look at other industry listings, too. *The Directory of Directories* should lead you to lists of companies in your industry that you never heard of. All are potential buyers of your talent. In making your assessment, you are likely to come to the conclusion that there are many more companies in some industries in which your present position can be found than there are in others. The *size* of each potential market for you is important to note as it will be helpful to you later as you develop your personal marketing plan.

WHAT IS THE GROWTH TREND IN EACH OF THE INDUSTRIES IN WHICH YOUR JOB TITLE MIGHT BE FOUND?

This question may be a little bit harder to answer than the last one, but not impossible by any means! The Department of Labor regularly publishes an *Economic Outlook* which covers many industries, for example. This may give you the answer you seek. Wall Street securities firms also provide long-range forecasts on the growth of many industries. These are available free from most brokerage offices. And, of course, your own insight into industries in which your job title exists will suggest that some are growing more rapidly than others. Your goal in answering this question is to try to predict whether there will be more companies in those industries that require your talents in five or ten years time than there are now (and hence more opportunities). Obviously, if you anticipate more new companies in one industry, you have more options personally than in other industries where the number of companies is decreasing.

Why is this exercise important? Let's consider a typical example. Assume you are an accountant. As such, your position is likely to be found in most industries—from computer peripherals to breweries. The future of these two industries, however, is vastly different. Were you to join the accounting department of a computer company, in five years time your options should be greatly expanded since information processing is a burgeoning industry. But, judging from the contraction of the beer industry, in five years time the number of job opportunities in accounting departments in which experience in the malt liquor business is an asset are likely to be far fewer than there are today.

Now you might be thinking that at this point in your career there's not much you can do to get out of your current industry and into a new one. If you've spent 30 years in women's wear accounting, this just might be the case! But for now, let's be optimistic on this score and assume you can break out of your rut. In this case, it would pay you—and every career person—to look at *all* industries in which your existing position is required. And it's worth finding out which are on the upswing and which are stable or declining.

WHERE ARE THESE INDUSTRIES CURRENTLY LOCATED? AND WHERE DO THEY SEEM TO BE GOING?

As an example, if you are a computer professional, you are no doubt aware that computer companies concentrate in the Silicon Valley on the West Coast and around Route 128 in Boston on the East. If you look closer, you'll probably find other concentrations of computer companies, too, on Long Island and in southern California.

If, on the other hand, your present position is found in energy companies, you know they are geographically concentrated primarily in the Southwest, with smaller concentrations in New York and Pennsylvania. Similarly, if the position you now have relates to the automotive industry, you know its primary concentration is in Michigan, secondarily the Midwest.

As you analyze the geographic patterns of each of the industries in which your position is found, the Dun & Bradstreet directory can again be of value because the SIC section lists companies by location. Knowing the geographical concentration of the industries which have jobs similar to the one you now have will help you in two ways: If you are adamant about the geographical areas of the country you want to live in, you can automatically eliminate certain industries from your personal marketing plan. And, alternately, if you are determined to stay in or get into certain industries, you'll know which areas of the country you should at some time consider moving to!

As you analyze the industries that might need you, keep in mind that not all concentrate, and that these concentrations change. For example, at one time New York City was a mecca for consumer products marketing organizations. Today, the concentration is in Connecticut and New Jersey, and, in fact, companies like Borden have moved as far away from New York as Columbus, Ohio!

WHAT'S THE PROFITABILITY OF THOSE INDUSTRIES IN WHICH YOU'LL FIND POSITIONS SUCH AS THE ONE YOU NOW HAVE? AND WHAT'S THE LONG-TERM TREND?

Finding this information out is also less difficult than you think! *Business Week* magazine and *Fortune* magazine regularly review the profitability of companies by category. Why bother answering this question? Because, if your existing position would be found in several different categories, knowing the profitability of each could make an enormous impact on your long-term financial success! As a programmer, for example, you could elect to go into a variety of different industries. You could, for example, seek to join a time-sharing information services company, a minicomputer manufacturer, a mainframe manufacturer, or a major company in any field with a battery of computers of its own. The long-term profit trends of each of these alternative industries obviously affects the number of people hired, salaries paid, benefit packages, and so on. This is certainly worth knowing before you undertake any personal marketing effort!

If you answer the five questions above, you should have an objective picture of the true universe for your talents as they exist today. And it's likely to include more alternatives than you may have imagined for your skills and experience. More importantly, taking the time to answer these questions will help you avoid two problems common to many career people: first, they limit opportunities unnecessarily, and second, they concentrate their career development efforts in areas that are likely to be less rewarding in the long-term.

However, in answering these questions, don't assume that all options are equally accessible to you. Some industries that might use your talents are likely to be far more difficult to get into than others. But that's an entirely different issue, one which we'll take up later on. The point of this review is simply this: Unless you identify *every* potential market for your talents, you might miss the one in which you could go the farthest and enjoy the most success!

INDUSTRY-EXPANDING EXERCISES

See yourself as a one-industry person? Have problems in developing additional employment universes? Don't despair! There are several things you might do to broaden your employment horizons beyond those which first come to mind. Three suggestions follow.

Read the Newspaper

Take a look at the Sunday help wanted ads in your local paper. Do so faithfully for eight weeks. Or, if you prefer, read the *Wall Street Journal* Job Mart ads Tuesday or the *National Business Employment Weekly* for this same period. Read the job descriptions thoroughly—not just the job titles. You may be pleasantly surprised! You may well discover that your job exists outside of your own company or industry. It might go by another title but it could exist just the same.

When you look through the ads, you may be frustrated by the fact that the level of experience called for may not mesh with your own or that the particular kind of experience might not match up totally with your own. Don't panic. The point of this exercise is not to locate a job. Rather, it's to help you discover different types of companies and industries that might use people with portions of your background. Once identified, there are ways to expand opportunities. (We'll get to those later on.)

Peel Back the Layers of Your Experience

The more experience you have in any one aspect of any one industry, the more you're likely to be thwarted in your attempts to find new opportunities outside of your narrow range of specialization. But it is not impossible to discover new options. The secret is to back out each specific element of your experience. It may well broaden your outlook!

As an example of this phenomenon, let's pretend for the moment that you are a plant engineer with 12 years experience working for a large foods processing company. Your responsibilities include plant maintenance, equipment evaluation, equipment installation, plant layout, and so on. Quite obviously, the most logical market for your background would be large foods processing companies. But if you back out your "foods" experience, you might very well find that your experience is appropriate to other kinds of process industries such as toiletries or even paint manufacturers. If you back out your major company experience, it might open doors to many smaller firms.

If you focus on each element of your job apart from the others, you might also discover opportunities in other employment universes as well. For example, your plant layout experience might be appropriate in construction firms or architectural firms; your equipment evaluation experience might make you a valuable asset to an equipment manufacturer—particularly in the foods industry. If you were to back out the word "plant" from your experience, you might open still other opportunities. Your electrical or plumbing maintenance experience might be appropriate to large office complexes, transportation facilities, or hotels where the management of non-plant maintenance personnel is required. While the most logical next step for a plant engineer with your background is with a foods processor, peeling back experience could help you identify exciting options. A career in transportation or hotels, for example, offers peripheral benefits that might well make it worthwhile for you, as a plant engineer, to leave the "straight" career path.

Make a List of All Your Functional Skills and Talents

Then ask yourself: "What industries could make use of each of these?" This review of the components of your job would suggest completely new avenues for you to pursue. For example, let's say you're a systems engineer who, as part of your job, makes presentations regularly to your senior management. Let's say, too, that not only do you enjoy making those presentations, but everyone says you do a bang-up job when you make such presentations.

If you forget for a moment that you are a systems person and consider only your presenting talent, it might open up many opportunities you never dreamed of pursuing. These range from executive selling to advertising agency account work. Possibilities range from public relations to customer service for an engineering firm and so on. It may be that you would never consider taking a position in these fields. But, for now, at least give them the benefit of the doubt. By including them as employment options, you can build yourself the largest possible universe in which to achieve long-term success.

Reread Your Old Resume

Chances are it mentions a variety of industries and jobs appropriate to several industries and perhaps buzz words appropriate to still other job markets. Be sure to include every career universe suggested by your resume in defining the total market for your talents.

One last thought in suggesting that you broaden your horizons as far as possible. It's been my experience that many of the executives I've worked with have entered industries thinking they would love them, only to find that they really hated them. The sad thing is so many stuck it out because they thought they should. One client of mine had three successive and unhappy jobs in manufacturing management. When he finally took our battery of aptitude and interest tests, he scored miserably in mechanical ability. In his eight years in these jobs, he never really admitted to this fact! He just kept trying—and not living up to his expectations for himself. So, open *every* avenue at this point in developing your plan. You have nothing to lose and could find a rewarding new career path in so doing!

chapter four

Assessing your current position in the success market: part one

Have you ever stood in front of the Shampoos-and-Conditioners section in a large pharmacy trying to decide which items to purchase? Your range of choices is enormous. If you haven't studied the options available to hair-care buyers—particularly female ones—take a look at this section the next time you're in a drugstore. It's a study in packaged goods competition!

Just for the fun of it, I recently counted these items in a local drug outlet. There were 55 brand names, 180 products (some brands came in different styles), and more than 300 items! (Some styles came in different sizes.) Buyers had literally dozens of benefits choices (from aiding oily hair to dyed hair to blow-dried hair, and the like), dozens more active ingredients choices (from simple lanolin to exotic zinc pytithone), a half dozen product format choices (from lotions to gels to creams to tonics), and still dozens more choices in container styles and sizes. (They range from plain Jane quarts to exotic, gold-stamped, prestige-looking molded bottles.)

In a very real sense, when you market your talents, you are in the same position as one of these items. Whether you are an engineer, a marketing manager, an accountant, or a purchasing agent—in fact, no matter what field you are in—you compete with hundreds or even thousands of other persons in your career field who, along with you, ultimately vie for the few choice spots at the top of the particular success ladder that you are climbing. And your competition comes in all sizes, shapes, and management and personality styles, offering a host of experiential and educational backgrounds and a potpourri of skills, intellectual capacity, and communications ability.

It is precisely because there is a telling parallel between the competition in each packaged goods category and the competition in each success market that this book proposes that you approach competition in your field in much the same manner as brand managers do in developing their annual marketing plans. This involves a two-step process: first, an assessment of the relative strengths and weaknesses of the major competing items as they now exist on the shelf; and second, development of practical, step-by-step strategies to improve the competitive position of the brand manager's own item in the future. As a marketer of yourself, you can undertake this same two-step process even though it is obviously harder for you to qualify the strengths and weaknesses of your major competition than it is for the brand manager who is able to scrutinize major competitors by observing them in any retail outlet or by purchasing products for laboratory analysis.

How do brand managers assess competition? Usually from three different vantage points. Let's examine each approach.

BACK LABEL REVIEW

This is the easiest and most straightforward of the three comparisons brand managers make of the key items competing in any category. When you consider that a good many buyers at the supermarket or drugstore read back labels to help them make key purchase decisions, this type of comparison makes a lot of sense. Generally this exercise involves comparing labels line-for-line by asking questions such as:

- Does my brand have a better-known active ingredient than others on the shelf?
- Does my brand have a patented ingredient? (Many buyers are impressed by patents, even though they're just a bunch of numbers.)

- Does my brand have a larger number of ingredients than others? (Some customers feel the more ingredients they get, the better the item will work.)
- Does my brand have an endorsement that others don't have, like Crest's use of the American Dental Association seal?
- Is my brand manufactured by a better known or more trustworthy company?
- Does my brand offer more quantity for the price?

Obviously, in analyzing your personal competitive position, you cannot examine labels. But you can do something very much akin to it. You can compare credentials with others in your field who are at about the same point in their careers. While it may take some digging to do so, you probably can find out how your resume stacks up point-by-point with representative competition. To do this, you'll ask questions similar to those brand managers consider such as these.

Do You Have More or Less Degrees Than Your Competition?

In many fields, an M.B.A. is a required ingredient for those whose goal is to make it to the top. Realizing this, many of my clients have gone back to school for their M.B.A.'s when their careers plateaued. Others have done the next best thing; they earned an A.M.P. (Advanced Management Program) certificate by attending a 12-week crash course at well-known business schools. In other fields, a technical undergraduate degree is viewed as essential even by those people whose job function is purely managerial. In one major conglomerate, for example, unless you are a chemical engineer, your chances of making it to the inner circle are automatically reduced because virtually every executive in this company is a chemical engineer.

Do You Have a Degree from the Right School?

While the education you obtained may be just as good as that obtained by a person attending a more prestigious school, yours may not look as good on paper. Many companies favor certain schools. As an example of this, Russell Reynolds, Inc., one of the leading executive recruiting firms, abounds with Yale graduates. (Its illustrious president is an alumnus of this institution.) If you attended a city college, your chances of joining such a firm would appear very slim.

This comparison does not belittle in any way the value of your degree academically. But it can help you objectively assess the selling power of this particular ingredient, since prospective bosses may well be influenced by it as they study qualifications to decide between you and your competition.

Do You Have Too Many Degrees?

This may seem absurd. How can one have too much education? But it is a very legitimate question. For example, people with a series of unrelated degrees give the impression on paper of being perpetual students. And that can hurt them. As another example, attorneys who don't practice law frequently raise questions in the minds of those reading their resumes. (One could easily ask why did the person go to law school if he or she didn't intend to practice law?)

The fact is that in some companies and in some fields, degrees can be an advantage *or* a disadvantage! Ph.D.s are considered eggheads in some organizations, and in others persons of stature to whom their colleagues offer extra respect! Again, in suggesting that you compare degrees with others in the field, it is to insure that you are acutely aware of how buyers of your talents may assess your back label versus others considered for positions within and outside your company.

Do You Now Work for a Prestigious Employer?
Did You in the Past?

In every industry, some companies are the leaders of the pack. Often it's the largest—the blue chip, Fortune 500 firms—that set the pace, although in some industries, small boutiques and think tanks are held with the same high esteem. Do you work for the biggest or the best in your field? For example, if you are an accountant, can you say that you are or were a member of a big 8 firm? To be able to make this type of claim gives you a leg up with both those potential bosses in your firm or prospective employers and executive recruiters outside your firm who consider company affiliation as important a credential as the school from which you graduated!

On the flip side, have you worked or do you work for what people might call a "Who Company"? This is the kind of outfit that when you tell someone you are working for it, they say, "Who did you say?" If you do or did work for a little-known firm or one not well regarded in your industry, you need to consider this back label ingredient versus that of your competition as you evaluate your chances for success. (Of course, you can always do something to strengthen your back label in the future, as you'll see later on.)

Do You Have a Prestigious Job Title?

If you were able to garner a nice-sounding title early in your career, it may help you attain better titles in future. That's because many prospective bosses are influenced by titles. This situation can be likened to a prestigious cosmetic brand such as Revlon being able to secure distribution in better department stores, while an equally effective cosmetic with a lesser name (say, Cutex) might be unable to secure distribution in anything but discount or drug outlets.

Similarly, if you are called a manager in your company while people in equivalent companies are called supervisors, your better-sounding title may give you an edge even though your work is identical! As a case in point, at one time Johnson & Johnson used the title "Product Director" to describe people doing the same job as "Brand Managers" in other companies. Several executive recruiters advised me candidly that this difference in title (not function) was worth eight to ten thousand dollars a year when they presented J&J candidates to their clients!

In some instances, a prestigious title can be more valuable than working for a prestigious company. For example, in a giant corporation like General Electric, an engineer making $60,000 a year could well be saddled with the title of "Sub-section Manager." (Such a title would create envy in this 380,000 person organization.) In contrast, an engineer with a similar background and making the same income, working for a little-known manufacturing company might well be called "Director of Engineering"!

The extent to which a prestigious title is better or worse than a prestigious company depends, of course, on the particular buyer of your talents. If you are lucky enough to have both prestigious titles *and* prestigious company affiliations on your back label, you really have the cutting edge!

Did You Have a Prestigious Title in the Past?

Titles can work against you! If you had a better title in the past than now, it could well bode problems for you in the future. Even if you have a lesser title now because you joined a larger firm, this decline in prestige may well lead to further declines unless you counteract this on-paper decline in your credentials.

A prestigious title can work against you in another way, too. If people within your field assume that your past prestigious titles make you too expensive to be won over to new positions, you may just not be considered for them. Again, recognizing this fact and doing something about it could be essential in order to move your career ahead.

Do You Have Certifications that Set You Apart?

In many larger companies, being a C.P.A. will give you the edge as you make your way up in the financial department. The noncertified accountant who is every bit as good with figures as the accountant who happened to have previously worked for a public accounting firm (and so took the C.P.A. examination) may well be out of the running for the positions of Treasurer of Chief Financial officer. The fact is, such certification may not help in the slightest when it comes to performing on the job! But it may well be the key to being promoted to certain positions! That's the back label difference you need to be aware of. In the personnel field, being a Certified Personnel Counsellor may make a difference. Being a Professional engineer adds stature in many engineering fields. (Such a certification does not require a degree, but rather a state examination.) The key question to consider is this: Do people in *your* field at *your* level of development have the same certifications you do? Or more? Or less?

Are You a Member of a Prestigious Personal or Professional Organization?

Do you belong to the University Club located in your city? Or to the Century Club? To any by-invitation luncheon club? In New York, it could be the Cloud Club or the Sky Club. In Norfolk, it's the Harbor Club. Such memberships may not reflect your personal stature so much as the stature of the organization you work for. In one such club, all executives—from the most junior to the most senior—are automatically granted membership as long as they work for the largest bank in this particular city. In most instances, however, membership is not that easy to come by and signifies either professional recognition by peers or social ties.

In either case, these clubs are elitist by definition. As such, membership in these órganizations is often impressive not only to other members who seek their own kind but to nonmembers who seek association with persons who have this type of recognition! On the other hand, to those who are turned off by snob appeal, membership in such clubs could even create a negative impression.

The important thing at this stage of your back label comparison is to identify which credentials you have versus others in your field at about your level of career development. Keep in mind that there are no rights or wrongs to any of these or similar back label questions. You are simply trying to codify the perception of you by people who might advance your career and to compare this perception with those with whom you compete.

LOOKING CLOSER AT THE REAL YOU

Make a list of all the facts that would be included on your own back label. Then ask yourself:

1. Which of my back label statements do I feel are stronger than others?

2. Have I taken full advantage of each of my strongest back label statements in the past? Which of these statements has helped me secure jobs? Which has helped me secure advancement in these jobs?

3. Are there any statements on my back label that I think aren't particularly strong?

4. Is there anything I can do now or in the future to strengthen each of the statements on my back label?

5. Am I willing to commit myself to improving one or more statements on my back label so that I have a competitive advantage in the future?

6. Make a list of all your peers in your current and past jobs. Which of these persons do you think has a better back label than you? Why do you say that?

chapter five

Assessing your current position in the success market: part two

The second comparison brand managers make involves the *total shelf impression* of their brands versus that of other brands in the product category. This reflects a review of size, shape, and color of both package and front label. The comparison also includes the brand manager's judgment of the relative sales value of each brand's name, slogans, or benefit claims that appear on the front label.

Obviously a comparison of shelf impressions is far less quantifiable than a comparison of ingredients, manufacturers' names, or quantity offered. This assessment is, however, probably more important since shelf impression, or "brand image" as it is sometimes called, is generally a more important determinant of purchase decisions than information provided on back labels. To make this second comparison, brand managers will ask questions like:

- Does my brand have a more eye-catching package than others?
- Does my brand *look* more upscale, more valuable than competing brands?
- Does my brand *look* like it contains more than other packages of comparable size?
- Does my brand *look* like it's easier to hold or use?

- Does my brand have a name that *infers* more benefits? Like Duractin nasal spray? Listerine mouthwash? Vaseline Intensive Care lotion?

Such package assessments are always subject to opinion, but brand managers try to make them as objectively as possible. In determining your own competitive position, it is critical to assess your shelf image versus others in your field—your size, looks, and so on—as rationally as you possibly can since ultimately *what you appear to be* has an impact on the value of judgments made about you and your competitors by those in your field who are in positions to forward your career. The questions that follow will help you do this.

WHAT DO YOUR CLOTHES SAY ABOUT YOU?

Amazing as it may seem at first, the outfits you usually wear to work affect your competitive position since they create an impression of you that is just as real as the impression created by your work performance.

For example, the cut of your wardrobe suggests whether you are conservative in thought or, perhaps, even old-fashioned. Large lapels and cuffs, narrow and bell-bottom trousers come and go. If you still occasionally wear suits with these features (or dress outfits with equivalent out-of-vogue styling), the people who work with you really can surmise only one of three things: that you are comfortable with old ideas, that you are unaware of new ones, or that you don't care about the visual impression your clothes create—at least not sufficiently to do something about them. On the other hand, if you make it a point to wear the latest cut from Italy or France, people may well assume that you are up-to-date or even avant-garde in your thinking or wish to appear that you are.

Your wardrobe may also suggest the part of the country you are from or associate with. (Piping and pearl buttons are distinctively Western in character, for example.) Or it may suggest the schools you have or wish you had attended. (The distinctive four-button Brooks Brothers model, for example, is a particular favorite of Ivy Leaguers.)

Wardrobe materials suggest things about you, too. Oxford cloth shirts are often associated with the Northeast and conservative business-people. Pattern-on-pattern shirting could peg you from New York or from a European cultural heritage. Wool blends are fashionable among business executives whereas polyester knits are considered downscale by these same wool-blend executives.

Colors, too, create a mental picture of you. Navy blue blazers are considered conservative and, as such, are frequently worn by executives in offices in which suits are the rule of the day. On the other hand, green blazers are infrequently seen in the office despite their immense popularity at golf clubs. Quite possibly this is because the owners of such jackets consider this color flamboyant. According to one leading fashion expert, light tan or neutral-colored raincoats are a sign that the wearer is upscale while the same coat in black suggests that the wearer comes from a lower class background.

Fit and condition of your wardrobe creates an impression, too. According to a survey by Robert Half and Associates, a leading employment agency, being overweight will affect your chances of getting job offers. Yet, you have undoubtedly seen businesspeople in suits or dresses that are far too small for them and which highlight the fact that they have grown out of their clothing. Suits and dresses which are too large look just as bad! Losing 30 pounds by jogging or dieting is certainly admirable, but wearing a size 16 collar when you are now a size 15 does not! Poor-fitting attire can't help but suggest something about the wearer's lack of concern for looking his or her best. Similarly, suits, dresses, and shirts with missing buttons, shiny bottoms, frayed cuffs, underarm or other stains, or deep wrinkles not only give a negative impression of the wearer but also of the way the wearer thinks.

Importantly, it is perfectly okay for you to disagree with the conclusions just drawn about materials, cut, color, and condition of a person's wardrobe! You are entitled to your opinion. In point of fact, what you and I both infer about other people based on their wardrobes is really not at issue! What counts is what people who can influence your future conclude about you versus your peers based on your attire. And here's the scary part: these important people in your life may not have ever revealed to you their feelings about what you wear! In fact, they may not have ever consciously verbalized their feelings to themselves! Nonetheless, you and your peers have created impressions with your attire that greatly color the impression created by your work performance. Thus, regardless of whether you personally care about the clothes others wear, it would pay for you to be conscious of this critical factor in your own success!

WHAT DO YOUR ACCESSORIES SAY ABOUT YOU?

Just as suits and dresses tell a story about you, so do glasses, watches, jewelry, ties, socks, shoes, briefcase, and the like. As a case in point, a psychology major at a leading university asked more than 700 students in one class to try to guess who the most studious classmates were based on pictures in the class yearbook. The psychology major concluded that if you wore glasses, your chances of being considered bookish were *ten times* greater than if you didn't, and the thicker the glasses, the more bookish you were considered to be!

Here is another telling example: our company is frequently called upon to help up-and-coming executives prepare themselves to take interviews with more senior people in their companies. Often our counsellors will suggest to these executives that their glasses or watches are out of keeping with the suits they are wearing. At this point, these executives usually respond by saying that they are only wearing safety glasses because they were provided by the company or that the 20-year-old watch they are wearing has sentimental value since it was a birthday or anniversary gift. These excuses are very legitimate. But they detract just the same from the overall impression these executives create, and we urge that more appropriate accessories be purchased.

As still another example, an executive recruiter once advised me that a woman executive who was the leading candidate for a managerial position was later turned down by the male hiring executive based on the fact that she was wearing avant garde rings on every finger during her interview. Obviously this was a sexist decision and not a fair way to select the best candidate for the position. Nonetheless, those bent-wire rings were the critical factor and cost this executive a job. The selection process in most companies is rarely or never completely without prejudice. It's a fact of life. Had the woman executive been more conscious of her shelf impression and its impact on her future, she might well have thought differently about wearing all her rings to the interview.

Wide ties, white socks (with a suit), and wedgie shoes can tarnish an otherwise positive impression. An accessory as small as a watch or tie clip can create the wrong overall impression of you—neither tie clips, tacks, nor collar pins are in vogue as of this writing. The brand of cigarette you smoke or whether you smoke at all adds a dimension to your shelf impression, too. Even your briefcase is part of your package since you walk into interviews or presentations with it. If yours is made of molded plastic or a cheap vinyl sheeting, it says one thing. A genuine leather case says something else. Is it worth investing in a $400 briefcase or a $250 watch? That depends on what your bosses and sponsors think of such items and how your accessories stack up with those of competitors. Later we'll look at ways you can determine what these people who are important to your future success actually do think about the accessories you wear.

WHAT DOES YOUR PHYSICAL APPEARANCE SAY ABOUT YOU?

Several studies have been made of the height, weight, and looks of top executives in top U.S. corporations. While successful business leaders come in all shapes and sizes, these studies conclude that tall, broad-shouldered, good-looking people make up a disproportionately large segment of this elite group that make it to the top. Some psychologists refer to this phenomenon as "psychological weight." These presidents and vice-presidents look like leaders and as such, were more likely to be selected by prior leaders to assume leadership positions.

You might argue that just having physical presence (as it is sometimes called) should not be used as a criterion in the selection process. Again, my feelings and yours on this issue aren't really what counts. What matters is that God-given physical qualities do have an impact on the fortunes of career people and as such, *must* be taken into account in developing your personal marketing plan.

Fortunately, some aspects of your appearance can be controlled more easily than your height or facial features! Your hair, for instance, is one physical feature which you can easily do something about. Our firm has worked with many male and female career people whose hair made them look far older than their chronological age.

In one of our outplacement seminars, for example, there was a 38-year-old sales executive who was prematurely grey. This individual never realized what this inherited feature did to his shelf impression until the seminar leader called for a vote. The result was that 27 out of 30 class members guessed his age at 48 or older! Immediately after the class, this sales exec bought some Grecian Formula hair conditioner. Five weeks later at a follow-up session, the instructor saw this sales executive. At first he didn't recognize him. The sales exec not only was 38, but now he looked 38!

Another example of this is a 53-year-old General Manager, whom I personally worked with, who had plenty of hair that he wore plastered back on his head. Not only did this style look old-fashioned, but it made his forehead appear enormous and barren. I suggested he see one of today's stylists—something he had rejected totally in the past. The next time we met, his hair was blown-dry rather than greased down; his thick hair was brushed forward, reducing his forehead in half! I asked him if he had any reaction to the change. His wife loved it. Just as important, at least ten people at his company told him he looked six years younger. "But is hair coloring or styling worth the expense and bother?" you ask. For this executive, forced to compete at 53 with other qualified people as much as ten years younger than he, the answer was an unqualified *yes*! Not only did he give a more youthful impression, but it gave him a much needed psychological boost to know he could compete in a tight job market.

Facial hair can affect image as much as hair on the top of your head. At one time, beards could all but do in an aspiring career person in any profession. Today there are still many conservative businessmen who frown on underlings who persist in wearing them although in some industries they are quite acceptable, and the well-manicured salt-and-pepper beard can make some appear more dignified or more authoritative than they might be without them. While moustaches are fairly commonplace, even they can have an impact on shelf impression. The well-tailored moustache that is seen in *Gentlemen's Quarterly* obviously projects an entirely different picture than the heavy, bushy moustache that may be rightly, wrongly, or unconsciously associated with certain ethnic groups. Our counsellors have suggested that droopy moustaches be trimmed at the corners for yet another reason: the wearer looks perpetually dejected as a result of the downturn at the corners of the mouth. Trimming such moustaches to be even with the mouthline has had a remarkable impact on creating a more positive image for the persons who wear them.

Experience has shown that hair can have an impact on women executives' success just as much as it does for men. One financial V.P. of a publishing company wore her hair in an ultrasophisticated french-twist. She looked so uppity that her new boss was instantly turned off by her.

A more relaxed hairstyle (and, incidentally, less makeup) gave her a far more down-to-earth and accessible appearance. Another female executive in her 50's wore her hair dyed brassy blond and in a style associated with people in their 20's. She didn't look that young; rather, she looked as though she were trying desperately to look that young! The point of these examples is simple: you need to assess your hair coloring and styling in the context of the overall shelf impression it creates for you and to compare this impression with that of your competition.

A poor complexion may also affect your chances for growth. As a case in point, our firm has suggested to many male executives—particularly bald ones—that they make a conscious effort to get a tan, either at the beach or by skiing, or if neither of these is possible, with a sunlamp. The results of tanning are sometimes astounding. Not only can a youthful glow take years off career people's appearance, but it can also provide them with a more active image as well since the tan voids the pasty look associated with people who never see the great outdoors. With female career people, the impression created by skin color is far easier to deal with, and our counsellors frequently suggest that clients go to an Elizabeth Arden, Merle Norman, or other similar makeup salon. These visits have resulted in healthier-looking, more youthful, and even more glamorous clients. In every case, too, clients feel better about their success chances when their complexion enhances their image, and as a result, project better total impressions of themselves!

You should consider other physical characteristics, too, in evaluating your self-impression. A paunch or beer belly may make you appear overweight even if you're not. As alluded to earlier, excess poundage *does* affect career people's success. Fortunately, there are exercises specifically designed to reduce both.

Jowls, large bags under the eyes, furrows, and deep facial creases may age you far beyond your chronological years. You don't have to live with an older image these days; 25% of all plastic surgery involves men who decided they didn't want to. This book offers no recommendation on this topic, but rather points out that the option does exist. Red, watery eyes or puffy eyelids may count against you. Even if these features are inherited, they may be taken as danger signals by executives concerned about possible drinking or drug problems. Tobacco-stained fingers may be far more detrimental to your career health than you can imagine. They may be taken not just as a sign of an individual habit, but of your background as well.

Even a healthy habit like jogging, when done to excess, can have a negative impact on your success chances. An emaciated appearance reduces your physiological weight despite the fact that it was come by in the name of good health.

Posture can downgrade your career chances, too. Stooped or rounded shoulders may negate the presence enjoyed by tall career people, while erect posture can add psychological inches to short ones.

Again, it may be that you do not wish to change the real you. That's a reasonable option. This book only suggests that you be aware of all that impacts on your career image versus others competing with you and factor it into your marketing position and overall strategy.

WHAT DO YOUR SPEECH AND VOICE SAY ABOUT YOU?

If you had the good fortune to see *My Fair Lady*, you know that Professor Higgin's special talent was determining the personal history of all people he met after listening to them speak for just a few seconds. This talent is more universal than perhaps most people realize.

Your speech patterns and choice of words may well reveal where you are from. Midwesterners are prone to pronouncing "boots" as "booots," for example; Bostonians pronounce "car" as "caah." Your speech may suggest where you graduated from college! It is said that Vice-President George Bush sounds far more like he graduated from Yale than was born in Texas. Your speech may reflect the social strata you were born into, as it did for Eliza Doolittle in *My Fair Lady*. As a point in fact, the continual use of "ain't," "him and me," and "we haven't no" cost an otherwise brilliant account executive a Vice-Presidency at a prestigious advertising firm I worked with. Your speech may reflect your religious up-bringing or current concern. Former President Nixon's almost nonstop use of profanity, for example, suggested he had long since given up his Quaker upbringing. And so on.

How important are speech patterns, accent, or idiom to your success image? Enormously! Why else would our firm have been asked by major companies to coach mid-management executives being considered for ad-vancement to higher levels? Why else would one of our clients, a South-eastern drug subsidiary of a Fortune 500 conglomerate based in New York, have asked us to coach their senior managers prior to their taking trips to seek approvals from headquarters in the "Big Apple"? (According to the Vice-President of Personnel for the Southeastern drug firm, "No one in New York took our executives seriously" because they didn't project a boardroom image when they made their oral presentations.)

The way your voice projects may be just as important to your image as your speech patterns. Some persons' voices naturally project authority. Have you ever spoken to someone on the phone and then later met with them personally, only to be surprised that the person was physically smaller than you anticipated? Other voices project sincerity. Walter Cronkite not only looks believable, he sounds believable. Still other voices convey friendliness and concern. Our Vice-President of Sales never sounds like he is selling. Rather, his voice suggests he genuinely cares about the needs of our prospects, which may explain, in part, his phenomenal success.

In contrast, we have counselled people whose voices and hesitant speech patterns project uncertainty, others whose voices suggest defensiveness even when they are trying to be frank and open, and still others who come across as wishy-washy, overly emotional, ingratiating, and so on.

The message in all this is a simple one: determine as objectively as possible how your voice and speech patterns, accent, and idiom impact negatively or positively (or both) on your career image, and if need be, take action to improve one or all of them.

WHAT DOES YOUR DEMEANOR SAY ABOUT YOU?

Recently I overheard a brand-new secretary in our organization whisper to another about one of our seminar leaders. "Doesn't he *ever* stop running?" she asked. In less than a day of being on the job she had formed an impression of this person that will probably remain in her mind as long as she works for our company!

While it may take longer for others to draw general conclusions about you based on your demeanor, there's little doubt that they *will* draw them. If your gait or reaction time (to, say, answering a ringing phone) is slow, others you work with may generalize and describe you as relaxed or laid back. If you rarely, if ever, crack a smile as you deal with business associates, you may well project an image of being overly serious. Or, as just plain unfriendly! Now you may be totally unconscious of whether you smile or not. That's not the point. Others will develop an image of you as being a cold-blooded person just the same.

On the other hand, if you kid around a lot, laugh out loud at the latest office joke, and play the office storyteller, key people may take you less seriously at business meetings even if you are earnest during them. If you become moody when things go wrong, are quick to flare up when a mistake is made, or shout at subordinates when an occasional error is made, you may create a long-lasting impression with key people that you are emotional, immature, or fall apart under fire. And this image of you could hurt your chances for advancement even if you are the nicest of persons when things are going well, which is probably 99% of the time.

Our firm works with a well-known consulting psychologist who developed a battery of tests to help people become aware of their personality traits. His tests are able to reveal whether a person is more or less defensive than others, more or less objective, compassionate, sensitive to criticism, tolerant of other people's ideas, decisive, cheerful, and so on.

This psychologist created his personality-testing device because in his experience, people with particular kinds of personalities did better in various business fields and job functions than others, and so he advises people with certain groups of personality traits to pursue or avoid certain career paths. Our firm believes these tests are valuable for yet another reason: they can help anyone who takes them understand the demeanor he or she projects to peers, mentors, bosses, and others.

How important is demeanor to your success in marketing yourself? Tremendously! As an example, Bob Johnson, one of the people our firm outplaced, was a research and development engineer with a background in physics, math, and computer science. In his field, Bob was regarded as a genius. He held a list of patents as long as your arm, and his company recognized this fact when it named Bob one of the 100 "Greatest Contributors to the Company" on the occasion of the company's one-hundredth birthday. (This award was no small thing; more than 400,000 people work for this company and to be selected as one of the top 100 contributors was a great honor.)

As you might imagine, Bob Johnson had a good deal of trouble understanding why *he* was outplaced from his company when he was so important a contributor. As part of the outplacement process, I spent four days with this genius. It became all too apparent why! As smart as he was, Bob was not smart enough to realize that he projected an I'm-smarter-than-you attitude that left those working with him resentful of the way he appeared to belittle their lesser contributions.

Another case in point: Jim Sorenson, a person we outplaced from a major chemical company, was originally hired by this concern to be groomed as the next Chief Operating Officer. Jim got caught in a political squabble and didn't make it to this position, and we were asked to train him in the techniques required to locate another suitable job.

During the course of his job search campaign, Jim had seven or eight initial interviews for positions as Chief Operating Officer in other companies but was never asked back for second interviews. Concerned about this, I reviewed Jim's tape-recorded practice interview sessions several times to see if I could find out what he was doing wrong.

At first it wasn't obvious since Jim is a smart, likeable guy. And then it hit me: all his answers to the interviewer's questions appeared tentative. Jim never responded decisively "yes" or "no" to any query. He gave the impression of being overly cautious.

I asked Jim why in this interview he seemed to lack the decisive quality associated with top management people. Was he, in fact, not decisive enough to pursue his goal of becoming a Chief Operating Officer? Was this why he hadn't been named C.O.O. at the company that was outplacing him? Jim assured me that in most business situations he was very decisive. But, he added, when he took the interview, he was very anxious to please the interviewer and thus answered questions in as accommodating a manner as possible. This explained why Jim appeared indecisive. I suggested to Jim that next time he try less hard to win over his interviewer and allow his decisiveness to come through.

As you might expect, Jim's next interview went far better, and he was called back the next day to meet with the Chairman of the Board and eventually joined this company. Incidentally, I suggested to Jim that he be aware of his accommodating demeanor in taking on his new assignment since he could appear indecisive on the job if he were too anxious to please his new boss.

WHAT DO YOUR CAR AND HOME SAY ABOUT YOU?

While these items are not strictly of a personal nature as speech, demeanor, clothes, and hairstyle are, they nonetheless have an impact on your shelf image since they are part of the total picture you create for yourself. In his book *The Hidden Persuaders*, Vance Packard suggested that Detroit in its golden age sold a good deal more than transportation; it sold prestige or sex on wheels. According to Packard, the person who purchased a Buick

Electra bought a visible symbol of financial achievement; the person who spent the same amount on a Corvette Stingray came away with a symbol of male virility!

Just as Detroit sought to provide you with symbolic automobiles, the car you drive into the company parking lot each day provides bosses, mentors, peers, and subordinates with not-so-hidden messages about the image you have of yourself and/or wish to project. A station wagon says one thing (family person and practical); a two-seater another (single and less practical); a subcompact, something else again (practical, concerned about money, and not interested in impressing anyone).

Similarly, if you drive a new car, you package yourself very differently than if you arrive in a clunker. Your choice of foreign or domestic automobile says something else about you as does your brand selection. (What type of person drives a Volvo? Would he or she be any different than the person who selects a Mercedes? Or Porsche?) Even the condition you keep your car in carries a message. (Is yours spotless and shining or always in need of a good wash?)

Just as your choice of automobile can affect your image, so can your choice of home if you regularly entertain members of your firm or industry in it. As an example, the executive working in New York City might just as easily choose to live in Manhattan or to commute from Brooklyn, Staten Island, Connecticut, Long Island, or New Jersey. If you were to ask anyone familiar with these alternative locations, he or she would probably paint totally different pictures of the financial backgrounds of the executive depending on which of these home sites he or she selected, and of the social and ethnic background as well!

The type of home and style of furnishings you select also say something about you. If you were to invite an influential peer to your home for dinner, would he or she come away saying that your taste ran to the traditional? The conservative? The offbeat? The ultra-mod? And would your taste in furnishings be compatible with his or her own? The more you use your home as a setting for displaying yourself to contemporaries, the more it affects the total picture you create for yourself. In a sense, your home is like the store in which a product is sold. If the product is only seen on the shelves of Lord & Taylor, I. Magnin, or other quality stores, it may be held in higher esteem than the very same product which is always on display at K-Mart, Zayre, or other discount outlets.

The questions discussed above might lead you to think there are right or wrong ways to look, dress, speak, and so on. Please don't draw that conclusion. The questions—and the discussion of each—were presented to you only to drive home the fact that all of these things may have an impact on the total shelf impression you make as a career person, and that each, by itself, could enhance or detract from your chances for success. No one aspect of your shelf impression is likely to cause you to rise to the top or fall by the wayside, but cumulatively, the package you offer the world and the back label potential mentors, sponsors, and prospective bosses consider in favoring you versus others competing with you affects your position in your success market just as these factors influence purchase decisions at the supermarket or drugstore.

WHAT ABOUT YOU?

Review the items in this chapter which influence shelf image. Then ask yourself:

1. Which of the elements that create my total shelf image are stronger than others?

2. Have I made full use of each of the elements that I consider to be the most positive facets of my shelf image?

3. Which of the facets of my shelf image have helped me to secure jobs or advancement in the past? How did they help?

4. Is there anything I can do now or in the future to make my total shelf image more positive?

5. Are there any parts of my shelf image that I believe to be less positive than others?

6. Make a list of all your peers in current and past jobs. Which of these persons do you think has a better shelf image than you do? Why do you say that?

chapter six

The third— and most critical— way to assess your position in the success market

One of the most successful packaged goods marketing executives I ever knew—a one-time Procter & Gamble brand manager and later V.P. of Johnson & Johnson—summarized the third and most critical way brand managers evaluate their products against competition with this thought-provoking statement: "J & J could probably package bricks and sell them to new parents *once.*"

This sentence may appear to be esoteric, but its message is crystal clear: J&J's reputation as a leading manufacturer of baby products is so strong that this company could probably put something as useless as a brick in a box, put a label on it, and promote it for baby's well-being. And, amazingly enough, it would sell to new moms and dads the first time! But obviously parents wouldn't buy it twice, because what they purchased didn't do anything for them.

This principle is just as true for career people as it is for packaged goods products. Unless you deliver something of value to those persons who are in a position to move your career ahead, you are unlikely to secure their long-term support.

To put it another way, your back label may earn you opportunities to provide value to sponsors and/or bosses (e.g., "Let's hire Bill. He has an M.B.A."). And your shelf image or package reinforces your sponsor's perception of your ability to deliver value (e.g., "Bill sounds so persuasive, I bet he is a great salesperson."). But in the end, if you want to move your career further ahead of your competition in your success market, you have to deliver more value to those people who are in a position to move you ahead (e.g., "Bill's $1,000,000 sale was a major factor in the 'Excellent' rating my Division received this past quarter.").

Given the importance of delivering value to sponsors and bosses, the critical question becomes that covered in the next section.

HOW DO PERSONS IN A POSITION TO MOVE YOUR CAREER AHEAD ASSESS THE VALUE OF WHAT YOU DELIVER TO THEM VERSUS WHAT IS DELIVERED BY YOUR COMPETITION?

The answer to this is: "In a number of ways." This chapter reviews the key ones. First, however, let's examine three things which many career people think are of great value to mentors and others in high places but which, in most instances, are of no value whatsoever! These include:

Experience. At first blush you'd think that experience is worth a great deal to bosses and sponsors. After all, the recruiting ads always seem to ask for it: "Must have experience in this or that." But experience is really an aspect of your back label. The name of the company you worked for, the years you worked for it, and so on are simply credentials. Such credentials suggest that you are *capable* of doing something of value for your new boss or mentor and thus help get you in the door or get you promoted in your company. But unless you then *use* the experience you have to *do* something that actually benefits your new boss or sponsor, in the long run your experience is really of no tangible value to him or her.

Skills. Again, it might appear that the more skills you have, the more value you would have for those in high places who are in a position to move your career ahead. In the long haul, however, unless you *use* your skills to do something that actually benefits your sponsors or bosses, your skills can be as meaningless as your experience. By way of parallel, if a high school all-star football player decides not to play football his freshman year in college, then his tremendous athletic skill is worth nothing whatsoever to the college coach who recruited him to play on the college team. The difference between *having* skills and *using* skills is an important reason why some career people fail to achieve the potential within them while other, less talented career people pull out in front of the pack.

Training. A great many companies place great emphasis on the education a person has when they hire people (e.g., "Must have technical degree; M.B.A.'s preferred."). But, as with experience and skills, unless the candidate puts this training to use to do something of value specifically for those who hired him or her, it is also of little long-term significance (e.g., "Jim told me he doesn't use his statistical training on this job.").

In sum, experience, skills, and training provide bosses and mentors with reasons to buy you in the first place and to have faith in your ability to deliver in the second. But they're not enough to sustain support for you. Only two things can earn you consistent promotions from bosses and repeated endorsements from sponsors: providing either corporate and/or personal benefits. Let's take a closer look at both.

CORPORATE BENEFITS

Simply stated, corporate benefits are those things you are able to do to significantly help the organization(s) you work for attain its (or their) stated goals. Four kinds of corporate benefits appeal most to bosses and mentors:

1. Increasing Sales

If you are a professional salesperson in your organization, and you sell more of your firm's products or services than other people in the organization at your level, you provide this first corporate benefit. Doing so should both increase awareness of you by the people who can influence your success, and increase, in most instances, the desire on the part of bosses and sponsors to support your growth and success in the organization. Hence, Corcorporate Benefits Axiom I:

In most instances, the more significant your contribution to the corporation, the more aware key people are likely to be of you, and the more anxious they are likely to be to promote your cause within the organization.

If you are a professional salesperson, you probably realize the truth of this axiom; the larger your personal contribution to the corporate sales goal, the more leverage you usually have in your own pursuit of success. But what if you are not in sales; can you still provide the first and most obvious corporate benefit? Absolutely, and to a larger degree, perhaps, than you may realize!

If, for example, you are in the marketing department and suggest a new promotional theme, you may contribute to your organization's sales goal as much or more than if you presented this promotion in a buyer's office. If you are in the accounting department and recommend a new pricing structure more consistent with the actual product or service costs in your company, and the new pricing schedule gives your sales force the ammunition it needs to underbid competition, you contribute to the sales of your company as much or more than if you had been the salesperson presenting these new prices! If you are a chemist or engineer and spearhead the development of a new or better product, you are making a direct contribution to your company's sales. If you are in customer service and smooth the ruffled feathers of a customer who is considering switching to your competition, you also are contributing directly to sales. And so on.

No matter what department you are in, the First Axiom of the Corporate Benefits principle applies: the larger and more direct your contribution to the organization's goal, the more *aware* bosses and sponsors are likely to be of you, and in most cases, the more inclined these key people will be to reward you with opportunities for growth within their organization.

As a corollary, the more *aware* sponsors are of your personal contributions to corporate goals, the more they are likely to aid in your personal growth. Failure to comply with this corollary is an important reason that many career people fail to achieve the success they feel is due them. What sometimes happens is that someone in the organization is credited with the corporate benefit provided by someone else (e.g., "A year later I discovered that my boss took credit for the Acme sale even though he didn't even participate in the presentation to them!").

More frequently what happens is that key people who might help advance your career aren't made aware of the contributions of any individuals to the achievement of corporate goals. A typical example is: "The review meeting focused on the critical issues of national and regional sales quotas. We didn't have time to review each salesperson's individual performance."

If you want to move your career ahead as far as possible, you need to make sure for yourself that the people who hold the keys to your progress do, in fact, learn the extent of your personal contributions to the achievement of corporate goals. This is particularly true for non-salespeople who frequently get little or no credit for their roles in making sales even though their contributions can be considerable! Later in this book we'll explore ways of making your corporate benefits better known. Let it suffice to say that if your sponsors don't learn of your corporate benefits (sales or otherwise), your chances of being rewarded are obviously more limited than they would be if they did hear about them!

2. Decreasing Costs

While not everyone in the organization or firm is in a position to increase sales, almost every career person has opportunities to provide the second of the four primary corporate benefits: reducing expenses of the organization. Again, Corporate Benefits Axiom I applies: *The more significant your contribution to the corporation (in this case, to cost savings), the more likely it is that key people within your organization will be aware of you and the more likely in most cases they will support your growth within the organization.*

If you are an engineer responsible for a process change which reduces the manufacturing costs of your company's product by $1,000,000 a year, you are far more likely to gain management's attention and hence a sponsor's support for your advancement than if you are an order clerk who discovers that you can actually save 30 minutes each day, worth about $1,200 a year, by standardizing the way you complete order-processing reports. By the same token, however, if you are the only one of six order clerks to turn up a savings of $1,200 a year, you are likely in most cases to secure greater recognition than the other five order clerks with whom you most directly compete for the support and endorsement of bosses and sponsors. Similarly, if you are one of ten engineers who each discover process changes worth $1,000,000 a year to your company, you are likely to receive no more recognition or support from sponsors than the nine other engineers with whom you compete.

Hence, Corporate Benefits Corollary 2:

> *In any single department of an organization, the people who make the most significant contributions to the corporate goals (e.g., increasing sales, saving on expenses, and so on) are likely to secure greater awareness and support from the next several levels of management directly above them.*

Importantly, just as you don't have to be a salesperson to contribute to sales, you don't have to be in the purchasing department to directly contribute to the reduction of expenses within your company. As a salesperson, you could design a routing system for yourself which reduces your travel budget. As a process engineer, you may come up with a modification in the blending process that eliminates one step and thus saves thousands of dollars. As a manufacturing manager, and hence a user of components, you may suggest a new competitive supplier program to the purchasing department that turns up a new source of components at 10% less than what your firm is now paying. As a controller, you may suggest a new auditing method that allows you to protect millions of dollars of overseas income against U.S. taxation. And so on.

Even if you are in the lower echelons of an organization, you can make significant contributions to the reduction of expenses. Recently I conducted a class for a group of secretaries, expeditors, and foremen who were being outplaced. Sixteen of the 17 in the seminar had made suggestions to their supervisors, and cumulatively they had saved hundreds of thousands of dollars! One secretary, for example, had consolidated ten office forms into four, which saved hundreds of dollars in paper and printing costs. One machine operator had suggested that the two holes usually punched into a metal motor housing be spaced the same distance from the edges of the housing. This simple suggestion eliminated the need for setting up two jigs as was previously done when one of the holes was a quarter-inch closer to the edge of the motor housing than the other. This quarter-inch saved the firm thousands of dollars in set-up charges, and the performance of the motor wasn't affected in the slightest!

In sum, in any organization, everyone at every level has the potential to provide Corporate Benefit 2. What makes the difference in many career people's rise up the corporate ladder is that they seized opportunities to provide this corporate benefit. They made it their business to look for ways to provide this corporate benefit even though it was not necessarily part of their job.

The machine operator, for example, could have kept punching each hole at a different distance from the edge of the motor housing, but she didn't. She took responsibility for finding a more economical way to get the job done. Then,

Corrollary 3: *Persons who go out of their way to provide corporate benefits usually advance more than others less cognizant of the need to provide such benefits.*

Doing what you were told to do usually isn't enough to put you ahead of the pack.

3. Reducing Time

When you think about the previous discussion, the first two corporate benefits have to be most important because increasing sales and reducing costs and up to what almost every organization strives for—profit! The fact is, however, that some organizations are not driven by the profit motive. Governmental, charitable, military, and other institutions are generally not profit conscious. But they are consistently conscious of the need to complete their missions in a given time frame. And this is often measured by how long it takes to do what needs to be done. So the person who works around the clock to make an "impossible" deadline gets noticed by those above him, as does the person who suggests processing a manual task on an available computer and thus gets the task done weeks sooner than anticipated.

Even in profit-driven organizations, saving time can be a corporate benefit. And that's simply because while you may think what you do saves only time, someone in a key position above you may translate the time savings into cost reduction. The auditor who proposes a simplified trial balance procedure may consider it only a timesaver, but the chief financial officer may think of this procedure as a way to reduce the number of accounting clerks on his or her staff.

This leads to

Corrollary 4: *The better able you are to translate time savings to money savings, the greater the support you'll usually receive from sponsors and bosses.*

Thus, if you are not in a position to determine just how a savings in time increases your organization's profitability, your hope should be that someone who can help you achieve the success you seek is able to make this translation on your behalf.

4. Improving the Performance of People in the Organization

When a maintenance engineer discovers a better way to oil the company's machinery, his or her contribution to the organization's profits is fairly obvious: the machines run faster and so save the organization time and they run longer and require less replacement, thus saving the organization still more money.

Improving the performance of people in the organization is as important—if not more important—as improving the performance of machinery. The fact is, however, that the development of people is a less obvious way to save an organization time or money. As such, it deserves special mention here.

If you develop a training method that takes less time to bring people to a desired level of proficiency than the previously used training program, you could be making a tremendous contribution to your organization's profit. If it takes one week rather than two to train ten assembly-line operators, you would reduce training costs by at least $2,000, if not more!

If you develop a program to teach new M.B.A.'s to become effective managers in three years rather than five, your contribution to your company could be vastly more important than training assembly operators. But the impact of your program is a good deal less measurable, and so it is more easily overlooked.

If you motivate a group of inspectors to be more careful when they check incoming parts, your contribution to company profits may be even less obvious. It could benefit your company, nonetheless, since the failure rate on these parts may affect the amount of warranty service that your company has to provide to your customers much later on, and even a fraction of a percentage drop in this failure rate could save many thousands of dollars!

What's important to keep in mind is this: improving the performance of people via better training, direction, or inspiration will ultimately save any organization time and money or have an impact on any organization's sales. Usually the relationship between the performance of people and profits is more subtle than the profits generated by an investment in a new machine or the development of a new process.

This leads to

> Corollary 5: *The less obvious the impact of your efforts on your organization's sales or profits, the greater the need for thought on your part to determine how your actions provide quantifiable benefits for your organization, and just as important, how you can communicate the quantifiable value of your efforts to bosses and mentors in or outside your organization.*

If you consider your present and future jobs as a series of opportunities to provide one or more of the four corporate benefits described above, and take the corporate benefits axiom and its five corollaries to heart, you stand an excellent chance of growth in any organization. Why so? Because in every corporation a large majority of executives who are in a position to advance your career (i.e., your bosses and sponsors) have themselves demonstrated that they are in tune with your organization's corporate goals. It stands to reason that these executives will seek you out if you, too, demonstrate in your job both the capacity and desire to provide the same kinds of corporate benefits as they have! That's why it's imperative in personal marketing that in each position you hold that you provide the greatest contributions to corporate goals that you possibly can. *And* that you do everything in your power to make people in positions to move you ahead aware of what you have done. It's that simple.

PERSONAL BENEFITS

As suggested earlier in this chapter, your ability to provide corporate benefits is one of two powerful factors in your quest for success. The other is your ability to provide Personal Benefits, the things you are able to do for bosses and others in positions to propel you ahead. All personal benefits relate to the fulfillment of one or more of seven basic human needs that have motivated people to action since they first inhabited the earth and that, incidentally, are the very same motivators used by today's marketing professionals to sell cars, homes, and yes, packaged goods! Let's take a look at each.

The Need for Wealth. Back in cave-dwelling days, people's first three needs were for food, clothes, and shelter. Today, people are more sophisticated. They need money to purchase food, clothes, and shelter. And the more money, the better, since the total amount of money affects the quality and quantity of these items the buyer can afford.

The Need for Safety and Security. Back in the days when cave dwellers wielded clubs to protect themselves, the larger the club, the more valuable it was. Modern mankind's view of safety and security has changed a good deal since then. But the need to secure one's body against harm, one's assets against theft, and one's source of wealth against loss is still a driving force in purchasing decisions.

The Need for Power. Have you ever noticed how many wealthy individuals seek elective office? The Rockefellers and Kennedys of this world are living proof of people's need for power over other people, which seems to grow stronger as one's need for wealth becomes fulfilled. A caveman fulfilled his need for power by persuading or forcing with a club people to subject their wills to his. People today use other techniques, but they are still motivated by the need to increase their personal power within the organizations in which they operate.

The Need for Comfort and Convenience. When some bright cave-dweller put a smooth, round rock under a flat one to reduce the effort required to drag it along the ground, he or she was motivated by a basic need to make life easier. One prime reason men and women are motivated to buy things today is because these things make life easier, less burdensome. Automatic garage door openers, home computers, washers, dryers, frozen foods, and cake mixes all are purchased because they save time and effort. Anything that reduces the drudgery of what has to be done will have buyers waiting in line.

The Need for Love and Affection. Homo sapiens aren't stand alone creatures. Throughout humankind's development, we have congregated in family units, tribes, villages, cities, and the like. If you have ever won-dered why so much of our nation remains uninhabited while the bulk of the population lives in overcrowded cities, one prime reason is because we human beings need the support and approbation of other human beings. This basic need for love is enormous and unending, and people will go to great lengths to win the love of the objects of their affection. Makers of cosmetics, clothes, chocolates, flowers, hair care items, and so on all know and use this basic need to enhance their sales. It's a powerful motivator in personal marketing as well.

The Need for Ego Gratification. Everyone needs to feel good about himself or herself, in a sense to love oneself. It's a universal appeal which has been used to sell insurance ("You're a good provider"), vitamins ("You'll feel better knowing you've done everything you can to protect your family's health"), education ("With these encyclopedias, you'll reach your full potential!"), charitable contributions ("You'll feel better about your-self knowing you have helped crippled children to walk again"), and so on. In summary, we not only want the world to love us, we want to love our-selves and believe we are good people.

The Need for Sexual Gratification. Since the days in which chauvinis-tic cavemen dragged off cavewomen to their lairs, human beings have exhib-ited a basic need for sex. The impact of this need hasn't changed much since then. While the manner in which men and women attract the oppo-site sex has grown a great deal more sophisticated, this basic need for sexual gratification remains and is a powerful motivator in many buying decisions.

In retrospect, it is probably fairly easy to reconcile your career progress with your ability to fulfill the four corporate benefits alluded to earlier in this chapter. It may be more difficult to reconcile your develop-ment with your ability to fulfill one or all of the seven basic human needs listed above. Experience has shown time and again, however, that success of career people at all levels is directly linked to fulfilling one or more of them. The five examples following hopefully will convince you of the impact of your ability to provide personal benefits to bosses and sponsors in your quest for success. In each example, the person does provide Cor-porate Benefit 1, an increase in sales. But, providing this corporate benefit is only part of the story.

Peter S. personally added 15% to the sales of the small electronics business he worked for—far more than any other salesperson in the outfit. His boss, the company owner, made Peter "National Sales Manager" as a result.

To an extent, Peter was promoted because he delivered Corporate Benefit 1. But just as important, the owner of the company recognized that Peter was instrumental in helping him to achieve greater personal wealth. The owner was hooked on making more money; it was only natural that he should offer Peter a major promotion to insure that Peter would continue to help his company grow.

Stephanie W. was also a top volume producer in her company. But unlike Peter, Stephanie worked for a Division Sales Manager who didn't own a single share of stock in the conglomerate that controlled the division in which Stephanie worked.

So why did Stephanie's boss make her the first female sales manager in the division's history? To a large degree, the sales manager did it because he believed in rewarding those who understood and delivered Corporate Benefit 1, an increase in sales. To a lesser degree, Stephanie's sales manager was probably motivated to reward Stephanie because her performance affected his personal wealth. (His bonus included an over-ride on sales produced by all the salespeople working for him.)

But fulfillment of another basic need was also a factor: Stephanie helped her boss achieve greater power in the conglomerate, something he had long sought. What happened was that Stephanie's boss had been competing for promotion to general manager in his division and had personally asked all of his salespeople to put out an extra effort in the first half of the year when corporate management was evaluating his efforts. Stephanie took the challenge to heart. During this period she put in more hours and put out more effort than anyone else in the division, and it was obvious she did so to help her boss look good. Not surprisingly, Stephanie rose from number 15 out of 20 salespeople to number one during this period. And Stephanie was rewarded by a promotion to sales manager shortly after the sales manager himself was promoted to general manager.

Joseph M. was one of the top producers in the dress manufacturing company which employed him. But instead of a raise, Joe was fired! In Joe's case, his boss was Field Sales Manager and was responsible not only for supervising Joe and a dozen other salespeople but also for making sales to key national accounts like K-Mart. In his position, Joe competed with his boss for the sales-versus-quota crown.

The fact that Joe outsold his boss probably wouldn't have cost Joe his job. But two other factors came into play. First, the Field Sales Manager was very insecure about his own position since his sales performance had slipped over the years. Second, Joe lacked the good sense to be subtle about his own career objective. (Joe told a few of his peers at the annual sales meeting that he was bucking for his boss's job.)

When Joe's boss got wind of this, he managed to find a minor infraction in Joe's expense reports. When Joe and his boss discussed this minor infraction, Joe raised his voice. The field sales manager immediately suggested that Joe might be better off working for another company.

In retrospect, Joe caused himself to get fired by failing to recognize that his boss was motivated by a basic human need to protect his job and his own financial security. In this instance, Joe's inability to recognize the personal benefit his boss sought (security) outweighed the corporate benefit (increased sales) that Joe fulfilled for his company.

Nick Z. had been a top salesperson in his company for many years, but he ranked in the lower third of the sales force during the last five annual sales contests. Nonetheless, the new regional manager made Nick the official trainer in his region—a prestigious position which earned Nick an extra bonus worth 15% of his salary!

Why did Nick's boss do this? Because the new regional sales manager realized that Nick had really helped him overcome the initial cool reaction towards him by the other 17 salespeople in his region. In this case, Nick was the only salesperson who went to bat for the new regional manager, openly asking his peers to give the new manager a chance. As an old timer in the region, Nick held an unofficial leadership position among his peers, and it wasn't long thereafter that the other 17 sales reps started showing the same kind of loyalty that Nick gave initially.

It was obvious to the new regional manager that Nick's personal support was a key factor in winning over his new sales team, and Nick was rewarded for just this. Thus, the new region manager's desire for love and approbation was a significant factor in Nick's new-found success. Nick delivered an important personal benefit to a person who held a key to his future. The fact that Nick failed to deliver the corporate benefit he was paid to deliver was largely ignored!

Lee N.'s sales territory was in the same city in which Lee's boss, the division sales manager, was headquartered. Lee's average sales performance was obvious firsthand to his boss. Also obvious to the boss, however, were Lee's easy-to-read and accurate travel expense reports. These consistently excellent summaries prompted Lee's boss to ask him to prepare the division's cumulative expense summary on one occasion when he was too busy to get to it.

Lee turned in an accurate consolidated statement days before his boss had expected it. As a result of Lee's initial effort, his boss asked him to prepare the division's consolidated expense summary each month thereafter—even though it wasn't really Lee's responsibility to do so. Lee did an outstanding job every month thereafter.

As you may have expected, two years later when Lee's boss was transferred to the company's headquarters to become a product manager, he recommended Lee for a new opening on the national sales manager's administrative staff—a headquarters position that put Lee in a perfect position to advance his career. In Lee's case, his ability to make his boss's life easier was a key factor in his personal growth. He advanced himself based on delivering a personal rather than corporate benefit (increased sales)!

Taken together, the five examples demonstrate how corporate and personal benefits can work together or counteract one another to affect a person's success potential in his or her company. In assessing your competitive position in your own organization, you need to consider how successful you have been in delivering both corporate and personal benefits versus others in your organization with whom you compete.

Did you help to increase your organization's sales? Save it money? Save it time? Develop its staff resources? And did you enhance your position by providing benefits not only to the organization but also to the people you worked with or for, directly or indirectly? Did you enhance your boss's own power base by letting him or her take partial credit for a new procedure you authored? Did you support your boss's plan of action with others in your organization, demonstrating your loyalty to him or her? Such loyalty is, in fact, a sort of corporate love and respect that is usually returned in kind.

Are your efforts making your boss richer? Better liked? Better known? Have you followed through with wholehearted effort even though your initial reaction to one of your boss's requests may not have been as positive as he or she would have expected? In such a case you demonstrate that you are someone to be trusted by the boss and make him or her feel more secure in his position.

Do you make your boss's life easier at every turn? A simple thing like completing expense reports legibly and accurately may be tremendously appreciated because it leaves your boss more time to do other work or be with his or her family.

If, after reading this chapter, you conclude that you have been less cognizant than you might have been of the need to provide either corporate or personal benefits, or both, then your cataloging of past benefits may have been of great importance because it could lead you to consider how you can provide both types of benefits to bosses, sponsors, and mentors in the future. And this may be the most important lesson to learn in moving you ahead in your career!

THE SPOTLIGHT IS ON YOU!

1. Make a list of each of the corporate benefits you have provided to the organization(s) you have worked for since you started your career. PLEASE NOTE: This assignment could take you several days to complete. Your list should include each specific thing you did that you know benefited your company.

2. Review your list of corporate benefits. Select the three most significant items on your list. Then ask yourself:

    a. Was each of your contributions recognized in the organization?

    b. By whom?

    c. How did your corporate benefit have an impact on your career? If your most important benefit did not help your career, why do you think it failed to do so?

3. Review your list of peers in your present position and in past positions you've held. See if you can recall any corporate benefits these peers were responsible for. Then ask yourself how the corporate benefits delivered by your competition helped them advance their careers.

4. Review your list of specific corporate benefits again. Put each of the significant contributions you have made into the four corporate benefits categories: sales, reduction of costs, time savings, and staff development. Then ask yourself:

    a. Have the corporate benefits I have delivered been concentrated in one or several categories?

    b. Could I deliver more corporate benefits in other categories if I chose to do so in future?

5. As you think about the list of corporate benefits you have been able to deliver versus those delivered by your peers, do you think you might be able to deliver more in future if you were more aware of the need to deliver such benefits in order to move your career ahead?

6. Make a list of each of your immediate bosses and other higher-level people in the organization you currently work for and in other organizations you have worked for in the past. Then review the list of basic human needs you might have fulfilled for each of these people. At this point ask yourself:

    a. Did I deliver a personal benefit to each of these key people in my career?

85

b. Which personal benefit (wealth, power, and so on) did I help the key people in my career to achieve?

c. What, if any, was the impact on my career development of the personal benefits I delivered to the key people I have worked for or with?

d. If I did not deliver a personal benefit to each of these people, could I have done so had I been more aware of the need to do so?

e. Were the personal benefits I delivered to key people concentrated in any one human needs category (i.e., wealth, power, love, and so on)? Should I be aware of delivering benefits in more or different categories in the future?

7. Did I ever deliver corporate benefits in the past which conflicted with personal benefits of those key people in the organization I work for now or those of the past? In what ways might my delivery of corporate benefits have conflicted with the delivery of personal benefits?

8. Considering each of the jobs you have held, have you been better at delivering corporate benefits or personal benefits? Why? Could you change that mix in the future?

chapter seven

Developing a buyer profile of the key people in your quest for success

By now you are familiar with the concept of shelf image—the overall impression that a particular brand's shape, color, name, and other qualities give to buyers. Listerine, for example, looks like it would be a medicinal product before you ever taste it; Janitor-In-A-Drum looks like it would be a heavy-duty cleanser. Surprisingly enough, buyers of branded products also have an image of their own. The marketing community generally refers to it as a buyer profile. To many people, the concept of a buyer image may seem odd at first. But if you consider the list of products below, you'll readily appreciate how easy it is to mentally categorize the characteristics of the purchasers of many branded items. For example, what mental impression do the buyers of these products bring to mind?

The buyers of...	are likely to be ...
Camel Cigarettes	_____
Virginia Slims	_____
Ivory Bar Soap	_____
Camay Bar Soap	_____
Bill Blass aftershave lotion	_____
Aqua Velva aftershave lotion	_____
Dodge automobiles	_____
Volkswagen automobiles	_____

If you are like most people, you *did* form a mental picture of the buyers of each of these branded products. Perhaps your profile of the Camel buyer was that of a hard-working, male, blue-collar worker in his 40's to 60's. In contrast, you may have pictured the purchaser of Bill Blass after-shave as richer and better educated than the buyer of either Camel or Aqua Velva. In each of these cases you formed a *demographic profile* of the buyer—a portrait based on age, income, education, or geographic background.

Your mental impression of the purchaser of Virginia Slims may have been far less concerned with the background of the person (male or female, young or old, rich or poor) and far more related to the mind set of the buyer. Yes, you undoubtedly visualized the Virginia Slims buyer as a woman. But you might not have pictured her at any particular age. Instead, your impression focused on her *psychological* makeup—she is "with it," assertive, an independent thinker. Likewise, your impression of the Volkswagen purchaser may have been related more to attitude than background. VW buyers are frequently pictured as economical, not influenced by style, not concerned with prestige, even hippy. This attitudinal picture is usually referred to by marketing people as a buyer's *psychographic profile.* And it is often the key in creating a sale.

Obviously, the buyers of many branded products have both a demographic and psychographic profile. The Ivory purchaser, for example, is likely to be a woman between 20 and 45 who is a believer in back to basics. The Camay buyer may evoke a picture of a somewhat older woman who is concerned with the world's reaction to her aging skin. The Dodge car buyer is most often categorized as a person who is older chronologically as well as old-fashioned and staid in his outlook. Of course, buyer profiles are not hard and fast. There may well be nonassertive, male buyers of Virginia Slims somewhere, or female Camel buyers who earn $100,000 a year working in executive positions.

Buyer profiles—both psychographic and demographic—probably represent people in the middle of the bell-shaped curve—the majority of users of any particular item whom you've personally known or become familiar with because they have been portrayed in a particular way in ads and commercials.

In personal marketing, as in packaged goods marketing, the better you understand the people who must buy you on your way up the ladder of success, the greater your chances of winning them over. Thus, the need for you to develop both demographic and psychographic profiles of bosses, bosses' bosses, and other people in high places in both your organization and others which you might join in future. In sum, it's not enough to understand what you have to sell (the things you've identified in the past three chapters); you must know what potential buyers in and out of your organization are looking to buy—the things that they usually prefer when selecting people for advancement.

How do you go about uncovering the personal preferences of these key people in your life? Obviously, you can't send them a questionnaire about their likes and dislikes in subordinates! Fortunately there's an alternative approach which can provide you with a pretty accurate picture of their preferences—a method, incidentally, that packaged goods marketers use regularly. And that's to study what these buyers have bought in the past.

The behavioral psychologists who conduct such studies look for consistent purchasing patterns. When they uncover them, they can predict with uncanny accuracy what buyers are likely to do when they return to the marketplace. As you conduct your own study of what the key people in your future are going to be looking for in promoting and/or hiring subordinates, there are six questions you should consider.

HAVE THEY TENDED, IN THE PAST, TO PROMOTE SUBORDINATES WITH SIMILAR BACKGROUNDS TO THEIR OWN?

A study of people in management positions in one division of a health aids manufacturing company, for example, revealed that the five top marketing positions were all held by persons who had previously worked as brand managers at Procter & Gamble. None of the other 15 or so brand managers who had joined this health aids company from Colgate, Lever Brothers, and other fine companies had been promoted to the top marketing slots in this division. You might think, possibly, that the former P&G brand managers were better performers. But in another division of this same health aids company, the top four marketing positions were all held by people who began their careers as salesmen at the old Vick Chemical Co. Why the difference? Because the V.P. and General Manager of both divisions had strong propensities to promote persons with backgrounds similar to their own. As you might have suspected, one was a former P&Ger; the other began his career at Vicks.

Previous business association is not the only such tie to look for in your analysis of potential buyer preferences. In one of the nation's most respected and largest investment counselling firms, eight of the top 25 management people graduated from Princeton. In contrast, as alluded to earlier, more than one out of four senior-level people at one of the most prestigious and largest executive recruiting firms graduated from either Yale or Harvard Business School. In both cases, the top executive in the firm—the most influential people in the outfit—graduated from the same educational institution.

Similar professions and/or skills can also be the basis of preferential treatment. At a New York-based conglomerate, for example, the last three CEOs were attorneys, and each was selected by an attorney. In another smaller Connecticut-based conglomerate, the three most recent CEOs were accountants and CPAs!

Even nationality has been known to influence corporate buying decisions. In one California paper products company which was founded by a Canadian, the directors of sales and marketing, research, and manufacturing all hailed from north of the border!

Equally astounding is the fact that in this day and age, religious preference can be a determinant in hiring and promoting decisions. Yet, in one hotel management corporation, the number of key employees with the same religious affiliation far outweighs this religious denomination's proportion to the population at large.

When you think about it, the fact that people in positions to advance the careers of others tend to select people with similar backgrounds is really quite logical. In the first place, when you—or anyone else—goes to the store, you are more likely to buy brands you are familiar with. And when you need a product you haven't bought previously, there is a very good likelihood that you'll select an item off the shelf that bears the same brand name as a product you do regularly purchase. The reason you gravitate to the brand you know is familiarity, and it's the basis for many line extensions like Vaseline Intensive Care lotion which was sired by Vaseline petroleum jelly and Ajax liquid cleanser which bears the same brand name as the scouring powder which preceded it to market.

Just as buyers trust the manufacturers of the brands they like to develop new products they can also like, so executives choose people with backgrounds (college, professional, religious, and so on) that they are familiar with. Whether these executives realize it or not, they are more comfortable with familiar names, and it affects their choice in people when they have no other way to assess their competence.

There's a second reason, too, why people with backgrounds similar to key people seem to get lucky career breaks so often. And that's knowledge of the key people. The executive who once worked at Honeywell, for example, is simply likely to know more Honeywell people through former business acquaintances. Similarly, he is likely to know more people who graduated from the same college as he did as a result of his attendance at alumni association meetings or to know more people who are members of his own church as a result of his own attendance at church functions. Likewise, you might expect him to know—or hear of—people with the same civic or sports interests as he has.

It's a fact of life that people in positions to advance your career may choose you simply because they have been made aware of your existence, because you both belong to the same professional society or other organization and so have a mutual acquaintance who brings your name up when the conversation turns to hiring or promotion. The sixth principle of successful marketing makes your past ties a powerful factor in your quest for the top.

HAVE THEY TENDED TO PROMOTE PEOPLE WITH CERTAIN KINDS OF PHYSICAL QUALITIES?

Earlier it was suggested that in some companies tall people are singled out for promotions, no matter what their backgrounds! And in other companies, people with psychological weight (large physiques) are selected for advancement irrespective of their actual contribution to sales or savings. Similarly, beautiful people are often favored for promotions. In such cases, the people who select them may feel that tall, handsome executives help the organization create the right kind of image with its clients. Even age can be the physical quality of preference. At a major publishing firm specializing in training materials, for example, no person under 45, no matter how talented he or she may be, has managed to secure a senior-level managerial position. (Many frustrated younger executives in this outfit have been bypassed in favor of older, greyer persons from outside the company.) In this instance, the president is 68 and feels more comfortable with people closer to his own age working directly for him.

Not surprisingly, age discrimination in promoting and hiring people often works in favor of younger rather than older employees. Within 18 months after a new 36-year-old general manager was brought in to take over one of the largest information processing networks in the U.S., he replaced seven department heads. All the replacements were under 35! Several of the older cadre who were forced out of this division went on to better jobs with other divisions of the conglomerate which owned this network. Several others, however, sued the conglomerate for age bias even though it was the new division manager's personal preference and not a factor in the other divisions.

Many physical preferences (like a bias towards short people or blondes) are totally irrational! Ed Rogers, V.P. of Personnel at N.W. Ayer and author of *Getting Hired* (an excellent book for people seeking their first jobs), told me of a seminar he once took which was designed to help people in hiring positions uncover personal prejudices which were unknown to them. At the end of this program, Ed discovered that he had been prejudiced against bearded, red-headed persons who smoked pipes. He didn't know why, he just was. Ed was concerned about his irrational preference until this instructor told him that virtually everyone has such biases. It is a fact of life that you need to deal with in planning your own career progress.

HAVE THEY TENDED TO PROMOTE PEOPLE WITH CERTAIN KINDS OF PERSONALITIES?

If you were to write up a short description of the people who have already been promoted by the head of your company, division, or department, would certain adjectives appear more often than others? Chances are that they would. Some executives surround themselves with hard workers—people they singled out for promotion because they work (or appear to work) 60 or 70 hours each week. In contrast, some executives favor people who make a conscious effort to develop friendships with people throughout the company. These executives are more comfortable with people who you might describe as politicians—the ones whose ability to motivate other people is far more memorable than their own personal contributions to profits. One division manager I know always promoted people who you might describe as street fighters—tough-minded defenders of their own points of view. This particular executive promoted Midwesterners and New Yorkers, Ivy leaguers and state university grads, handsome people and ugly ones. The single common denominator among the people working directly for him was an attitude of "I'll do it your way only if you can convince me I shouldn't do it mine!" In this particular instance, the general manager worked for a company which sells branded undergarments. It's a tremendously competitive field, and in his judgment, being a street fighter was precisely the attitude he felt was necessary to survive in this business.

The mental picture you have of people who have succeeded with your company may not necessarily be flattering. It may be that talkers advance much faster than doers. Or it could be that weak people seem to get promotions rather than strong, independent people. (Some bosses are just plain uncomfortable with strong contenders for their jobs working for them so they surround themselves with people who are competent but who you'd never classify as bell ringers.) It isn't important that the picture you have of successful people in your company be a positive one—only that it be as accurate as you can make it.

HAVE THEY TENDED TO PROMOTE PEOPLE PRIMARILY BECAUSE OF TIME-IN-GRADE?

Some executives favor old timers and can be counted on to promote on a "first in, first selected" basis. Everyone in such companies must punch their ticket at every station in order to make it up the corporate ladder. In contrast, in other companies, people in high positions constantly hire from the outside no matter how good the homegrown talent. In this case, these executives believe that new is better, that the longer an employee is on board, the less valuable he or she is to the organization. And so, everyone who works for them has a better shot at advancing his career in his or her first year after joining the company than in any year thereafter!

DO THEY TEND TO PROMOTE BASED ON SELECTED PERFORMANCE QUALITIES?

Your portrait of people who have been selected for advancement in your company may reflect people who are the best at some area of work measurement. They may be the best organizers, the best problem solvers, the most persuasive in dealing with others, the most creative, and so on. As you create portraits of those who have been promoted—especially those who are promoted consistently—keep in mind that there is no right or wrong set of qualities required for advancement, no single guideline within a particular company or industry. Personal preference is what makes for people success just as it does for brand success.

The critical issue, therefore, is to assess the personal buying preferences among the people who hold the keys to your own future—bosses, their bosses, and other influential people in your organization. The more complete your demographic and psychographic profiles of the kinds of people who seem to advance further in your organization or industry, the better able you'll be to use this knowledge in your own personal marketing program.

ARE THERE ANY COMMON DENOMINATORS AMONG THE PEOPLE WHO HAVEN'T MOVED AHEAD IN YOUR ORGANIZATION?

It's quite possible that you aren't personally familiar with many of the people who have moved up quickly within your organization, and so it is difficult for you to form a composite mental picture of the kind of qualities that appeal to those in positions to advance your career. If this is the case, it might pay to take a closer look at those people you know who failed to get promoted when you thought they might be eligible or who lost their jobs for reasons other than cause. They may all have had similar backgrounds, personalities, physical qualities, work performance attributes, and so on. If your review of people who didn't make it up the corporate ladder reveals that they do share common features, it could turn out to be just as valuable to you as your review of people who did make it to the top! If you don't know enough people who are moving either up or out to form judgments of either category, you might consider just comparing the ones you do know in each situation.

As you make your analysis of people who didn't advance in your organization, you may find yourself a little confused. One or more of the people who failed to make it up the ladder in your outfit should have succeeded based on the answers to the five questions outlined earlier! These people do have backgrounds similar to those in positions to promote them. They do have the physical qualities found in others who have been promoted. They do have personalities which mesh with others who have been advanced, the necessary time in grade, and in your judgment, the required performance characteristics! What, then, caused them to fail? In virtually every case in which seemingly good people bomb out, it's for one of two reasons. And both deserve your attention.

They Provided Your Organization with the Corporate Benefits Necessary to Succeed But They Did Not Deliver the Personal Benefits Sought by the Decision Makers

Consider these examples:

Gary N. was the best marketing strategist in the brand management group, with a background similar to the top people in his organization. His assessments of promotional plans was right far more often than those of anyone in the outfit. Even so, he didn't get promoted and eventually left. The reason: Gary intimidated his superiors by calling their attention to the fact that his recommendations had been ignored each and every time he was right and his bosses were not. Gary failed to realize the importance of providing personal benefits (in this case, ego gratification and the need for job security). Thus, despite Gary's obvious ability to provide corporate benefits, his insensitivity to personal benefits blocked his advancement.

Wally, R. was the most brilliant research scientist at an industrial chemicals company. He went to the right schools. He dressed like his mentors, and so on. His individual contributions were recognized throughout the company. But for years he was overlooked for promotion. The reason: at every meeting Wally attended, he automatically played devil's advocate, discussing the cons of every issue. Even when the issues were small ones, Wally found ways to complicate the discussion by raising obscure points that only someone as intellectually gifted as he could uncover. As a result, Wally impeded the decision-making process while all the time he thought that he was being of genuine value to his organization! But he failed miserably in delivering on the personal benefit of making life easier and more convenient for the people he worked for. And one benefit offset the other in the minds of those who were key to Wally's future. In marketing yourself, recognizing what turns your buyers on is critical to the sale.

They Delivered Corporate Benefits, But They Failed to Project an Image That They Had the Capacity for Delivering Such Benefits at a High Level in the Organization

Consider these examples:

John K. was one of the best young copywriters in one of the largest advertising agencies in the world. And his background was impeccable. Not only did he have an undergraduate degree in English, but he held an M.B.A. from a prestigious school, something admired by everyone in the agency. But John always missed being promoted to a managerial position. One reason: he had a high tenor voice that seemed to crack as he presented his creative approach to senior management. John just didn't sound authoritative. Another reason: his remarkably boyish-looking face and slight body. He appeared and sounded too unassuming to be considered for a management role! Eventually John K. gained weight and went to a voice coach to try to alter his image. Even so, he had to join another agency before he could get promoted to a supervisory position. His unassuming image at the first agency he worked for was too ingrained to be changed.

Mack D. was promotion director for a large publishing firm and was the most logical contender for the general manager's slot when the general manager retired. His track record of developing successful promotional campaigns was very much recognized by the general manager, who earlier in his career had been promotional director at this firm. What's more, Mack's department was extremely well-organized, and the people who worked for him held him in very high regard. Among the possible choices for the general manager's slot, Mack was seemingly the most logical. Nonetheless, he didn't get it. There were probably several reasons: thick glasses, a club foot, and a reluctance to make difficult decisions which caused him to put them off for as long as possible.

In the end, the general manager chose a successor from the outside because he just didn't think Mack looked like a general manager. (Mack limped slightly and looked a little like a bookworm.) This image was the straw that broke the camel's back. Those who knew the general manager well were convinced he would have lived with Mack's lengthy decision-making approach had Mack just projected the demeanor of a general manager. But he didn't.

The preceding examples illustrate how important the first two principles of personal marketing really can be! Gary and Wally delivered benefits to prospective buyers, but not without drawbacks. Like Anacin, which relieved headaches but upset stomachs, these two individuals failed to fulfill Corollary 1B of the first principle of marketing. Similarly, John and Mack didn't get people to believe in their ability to deliver corporate benefits, and like Micrin mouthwash and P&G's detergent with nonobvious whiteners, neither John nor Mack *sustained the image of performance* that their prospective buyers sought for the long run. In failing to fulfill the second principle of marketing, they limited their opportunities for long-term success even though, on the surface, they matched up to their buyers demographic and/or psychographic preferences.

In concluding this chapter, there are two thoughts to keep in mind. First, the better your profiles of prospective buyers of your talents, the more likely you are to attain the success you seek. Second, developing accurate mental pictures of the people who could play a role in your future will take a great deal of effort on your part. There's no way around it.

How should you go about developing these profiles? The easiest way is to begin with your boss—the person you work for regularly and who holds the key to your immediate future. Then attempt to create profiles of former bosses who still might be in a position to help you in your career. Next, profile your peers who you believe could be on the rise, the ones who you think could someday be in a position to catapult you ahead. After you've become adept at making profiles, try researching your bosses' boss, and his or her boss as well. You can probably find out something about these people's physical size fairly easily. Determining their backgrounds, personalities, and functional buying preferences could be a good deal harder.

In this regard, you may find your company's monthly newsletter, quarterly magazine, or other house organ can be of real value. Feature stories about your bosses' boss or write-ups about his or her promotion may well include information on training and earlier job histories, as well as his or her viewpoints on business and people. You might also ask your friends to join you in a team analysis of the key people in your company. (Your friends might also benefit from knowing more about these executives.) Together you may be able to develop a mental picture of these buyers that you might not be able to create independently.

Keep in mind, too, that some of the very top people in your company may be written up in *Standard & Poors Directory of Corporate Executives* or *Who's Who in Business*, both available at good business libraries. You might also want to read the foreword to your company's annual report. It could provide valuable insights into the thinking of the president and board chairman of your company. (Such information is as valuable to employees as it is to stockholders!)

If you have the opportunity, try to read articles about your company that appear in business magazines and newspapers. (*Dataquest's F&S Business Periodical Index* can help you locate such articles, and these may well include profiles of key people.) You might also want to find out if the public relations or stock relations departments of your company have copies of speeches made to the business or financial communities by people in your company. These may contain clues as to their buying preferences. If you deal with a stockbroker, he or she may have 10K reports. These sometimes profile key people within an organization.

Once you get into the habit of developing buyer profiles of the people who could help you move ahead, you might want to expand your file to include key persons in competitive organizations that you might someday join. There is more about how you can identify them in upcoming chapters. But this extra step is often worthwhile since the top people in your industry may well set the buying preferences for everyone in their companies. Let it suffice to say that the better you understand what drives potential employers, the better your chances of developing marketing plans to get them to buy you!

SOME THOUGHTS FOR THE PERSON
IN THE MIRROR...

1. Think of several products or brands you never buy. What is your image of buyers of these products? Develop a demographic and psychographic profile of them.

2. Considering schools, business affiliations, certifications, nationality, religion, and so on, who in your department has most in common with your boss? Why do you say that?

3. Considering height, weight, age, features, and the like, who in your department has most in common with your boss? Why do you say that?

4. Considering personality (fun-loving, serious-minded, etc.), who in your department has most in common with your boss? Why do you say that?

5. In your company, do most people have to earn their stripes (serve time in grade) before they are considered for promotion? Are there exceptions? Why do you think these exceptions were made?

6. What performance qualities do you think your boss favors? Why do you say that? Who in your department best matches up to these performance preferences of your boss?

7. How could you find out more about the buying profiles of the key people in your company?

chapter eight

A strategy for developing your full potential

PRODUCT IMPROVEMENTS AND SUCCESS

There's an old adage that says "Never tamper with success." But in packaged goods marketing, it doesn't seem to apply. Brand managers have altered, added to, and subtracted from successful brands again and again to keep them successful and to give them greater potential for future success. Some examples:

Anacin. This product underwent several formula changes, the most noteworthy of which was the removal of phenaticin, a pain-relieving ingredient which developed bad press after researchers associated it with cancer, and at the same time, an increase in its aspirin content. This latter addition was the basis for Anacin's claim that it had more of the pain reliever doctors recommend most, one of the most successful ad campaigns in analgesic history.

Ivory Soap. After more than a half century of being sold in an oversized laundry bar which consumers broke in two, a personal-size bar of

Ivory was introduced when Ivory's marketing managers realized that it was no longer being used primarily in the laundry, but rather as a facial soap. Incidentally, Ivory packaging has undergone many subtle changes in its eighty plus years on the market, and today's package is far more cosmetic and far less hardworking than the original package that supported Ivory's laundry soap image.

Colgate toothpaste. Colgate added MFP, a fluoride ingredient, when its sales were significantly cut into by Crest, the first anticavity toothpaste with Floristan. Unfortunately for Colgate, the new fluoride ingredient made Colgate bitter. Thus, more recently, Colgate announced it had a new flavor that the marketing managers hope is more palatable.

Fab. This product was introduced originally as a detergent, and its original claim.was that it did not leave a soap scum in the wash. In the years since its introduction, Fab added fluorescers (for increased whitening power), a lemon scent (to make clothes seem fresher), borax, a special rinsing agent (to make clothes feel softer), and within the last year, a new antistatic ingredient (to prevent clothes from clinging during cold weather).

There's a message in all these changes and the countless other subtle and not so subtle modifications that have occurred in the formulation and packaging of America's favorite brands. This message is that no product, no matter how successful, can afford to rest on its laurels. Improved effectiveness, improved aesthetics, and improved image all are legitimate reasons for upgrading and updating brands. Whether such action is to catch up to new competition or to get ahead of existing competition, no product —not even the most successful—can afford to ignore the possibility that it may require minor or major modifications in order to compete.

PRODUCT IMPROVEMENTS
AND PERSONAL MARKETING

Product improvements programs are just as important in personal marketing as they are in packaged goods. Investing time, energy, and money to make yourself as attractive a competitor as you can be in your success market is critical if you are to get all you can out of life. Studies of rate page for each action category with a comment from you (even if it's just "This category isn't appropriate to my goals for the coming year"), you are at least insuring that you have, in fact, considered the category and haven't inadvertently overlooked an opportunity for moving your career forward.

Each of the action category pages of your personal marketing plan should detail specific action programs in each category that you plan to undertake as part of your overall strategy. Name names and places, cite organizations and courses, and so on that these programs involve. If there are several action programs within each action category, indicate the priority you place on each in order to be sure that you tackle the most important ones first. And if you plan to undertake several sequential action programs within each action category, include a timetable showing when you anticipate completing each of the programs involved. This way you'll be able to check your progress periodically throughout the year to make sure that you are keeping pace with the action programs included in your plan.

The value to you personally of developing separate action category pages in your plan and listing specific action programs that apply to each category should become obvious as you review the ten action categories that follow.

A. Corporate Benefits Delivery

On this action category page, you would list all the specific action programs that you are currently working on or that you intend to begin and/or complete within the next 12 months. This is not the place to describe your job functions. They are a given. It is the place to outline the projects you personally intend to undertake as part of your job function that you believe will deliver extra sales or savings to your organization, will save your organization time, or will increase its long-term effectiveness. If you are in manufacturing supervision, for example, you might list things like:

1. *Undertake conveyor-belt study and recommendation.* (Show boss how we could eliminate duplicate handling as a result.)
2. *Write up new employee introduction pamphlet.* (This would eliminate some mistakes that new employees always seem to make. Possibly, I can sell the boss on having all supervisors in department use it.)

the average lifetime wages of people who have completed a four-year college degree versus those who have only a high school education make this point abundantly clear. You can anticipate earning half a million dollars more during your total working career if you have committed just four years of your life and $20,000 or so in securing a sheepskin!

And the payoff usually goes far beyond money. If you have the intellect to handle greater challenges than are generally available to people with only a high school education, you are likely to find a college-based career vastly more rewarding. Moreover, your circle of friends is likely to be more exhilarating and worldly. And since your income is far greater, you are likely to enjoy more day-to-day conveniences and more leisure time pleasures than your classmates who had the capacity for growth but who, for one reason or another, elected not to invest at least in a college education.

The fact is that personal development is a lifetime process and does not stop with college or even graduate school. The case that follows should convince you of this. Recently one of our outplacement clients, an appliance manufacturer, let go about 25 mechanical engineers, all of whom were in their late 30's or 40's. After reviewing the records of these individuals, I was somewhat surprised that they were losing their jobs. Each of them was a college-educated, hardworking individual. So I asked the personnel director why they were being let go. I was told that today the need for mechanical skills has been replaced by a need for electronic skills as our client shifted from servo to electronic switches on its product lines. "Couldn't these individuals be retrained?" I asked. Sad to say, I was told it was too late to begin this two- to three-year process.

Now you might argue that the company could have foreseen this shift to electronic controls earlier, making such a retraining program possible. It didn't. But is this the company's responsibility? Not really. These engineers could have kept pace with developments in their field. Had they done so, they would have known their skills were growing less and less valuable. More importantly, they would have had the time to learn new skills on their own so they would be as valuable to their company today as they were when they graduated from college. Even sadder is the fact that these individuals were replaced by engineers 15 years their junior. Recent schooling made the newcomers desirable employees, not their work ethic or knowledge!

From my perspective, this case history was clearly not a case of age discrimination, but a genuine skills mismatch which need not have taken place had these individuals made self-development a life-long pursuit, rather than one which lasted only into their 20's.

CORNERSTONES FOR STRATEGIC SELF-DEVELOPMENT

The first cornerstone in your strategy for fulfilling your full potential has to be this: *Make self-assessment an ongoing assignment.* In packaged goods marketing, you cannot hope to compete using last year's product when this year's product is a better one. In building your career, the same holds true. And this is so whether you pursue a career in medicine, law, advertising, production, business administration, or engineering. As a case in point, at the prestigious Harvard Business School back in 1957, you could not graduate unless you could quantify business decisions with the aid of a slide rule. Today you cannot graduate unless you can program computers in at least two computer languages.

At this juncture, you might raise this legitimate question: "At some time in my life, won't I prefer to devote more attention to my family and personal interests than to continue to invest in developing my professional skills for a future career payoff?" More than likely! But if you make it your business to assess yourself objectively against competition each year, you will know when you are losing ground to competitors. At that time, the choice is yours to continue to grow in your field or to opt for securing your satisfactions in nonwork arenas. The point is that if you assess your competitive status regularly, you'll know what self-development is necessary to remain ahead of competition, and therefore, how much effort and time this requires. Then you can decide if it's worth it. More importantly, you won't let yourself fall into a noncompetitive position that makes pursuit of your original career goals impractical.

The second cornerstone of strategic self-development is this: *Be as objective as possible in your appraisal of your competitive position.* Many an outplaced client has said to our counsellors that he or she thinks it is unfair that he or she has been let go while some younger, less experienced individual was moved ahead in the organization. This kind of reasoning isn't logical, and one case history should drive this home. Albert Santucci was an individual in his midforties with a background in computer operations and data processing sales. For six of the past eight years, Al had been responsible for the entire data processing center at a $300,000,000 chemical manufacturing company. But for the last two of these eight years, Al's responsibilities had been reduced to managing just the computer operator's functions (entering data, scheduling data processing time, etc.). At the time Al's responsibilities were reduced, he was told by his boss that he wasn't as knowledgeable about current programming and systems techniques as he should be and henceforth he would report to one of his subordinates who had a better understanding of these areas. At that time the subordinate was given responsibility for the entire data processing center that Al had managed.

Was Albert Santucci's outplacement two years later really unfair? Had Al been the least bit objective about his competitive position at the time of his demotion, he would have realized his inadequacy in programming and systems had to jeopardize his career at some future date. At that point, Al Santucci had two choices: to find a position which did not require updating his systems knowledge and skills or to learn these skills to remain competitive. Because he was not objective about his competitive position at that time, Al took no action, and of course, lost his job.

In previous chapters, you were encouraged to assess your current competitive position from several perspectives—your capability in providing needed corporate and personal benefits, your credentials, and your overall image as perceived by your current boss and potential sponsors inside and outside your company. What wasn't suggested then is that you need to make this kind of assessment regularly and very critically. Unless you know your competitive strengths and weaknesses currently and in the foreseeable future, you can't make strategic plans for emphasizing your strong suits, enhancing the areas in which you have the greatest potential for growth, and most important, ways of correcting those areas of your personal product and package that are likely to thwart your chances for success.

OPTIONS FOR SELF-DEVELOPMENT: TRADITIONAL EDUCATION

What options are open to you for building on your strengths and reducing the impact of the chinks in your armor? For most people, more schooling has been the standard answer. "If only I had an M.B.A. degree, I'm sure I could get my stalled career going again," is a comment we hear again and again from people who are sent to us for career assessment. Or, "I wish I had pursued that masters in chemical engineering instead of starting to work with only my bachelor's degree. I wonder if I shouldn't go back to school to get it." Certainly the extra sheepskin is an answer. But it may be an overly simplistic one.

If you think that additional schooling may possibly help your career, it would probably pay you to analyze why you think this is the case and what specifically you hope schooling will do for you. For instance, are you considering a return to school because *your credentials aren't as good as your competition*? If that's the case, then you may want to ask yourself several other related questions. For example:

Is the Name of the School Important?

If the name of the school is not important, then it would probably pay for you to look for the easiest or quickest source of an extra degree available to you. This could even be a degree you secure by mail (more about this in a short while). If, on the other hand, where you get that extra educational credential is more important than the credential itself, then perhaps the masters you thought you needed isn't really what you needed after all. Many highly successful executives, for example, have opted instead for an Advanced Management Program (AMP) certificate from a prestigious school and been helped enormously by it (more about this, too, in a few moments).

Is Technical Proficiency the Issue?

Do you feel you are not as technically proficient as others who compete with you for recognition from your boss and from potential menters? If this is the case, then going after a degree isn't really the best alternative. Quite often the requirements for a degree include courses that have very little utilitarian value on the job. One career person I recently worked with planned initially to pursue a masters degree in computer science because her analysis of her competitive position in her company indicated other financial analysts outclassed her in using the computer in their work. After discussing the alternatives with one of our counsellors, she decided what she really needed was a few good courses in computer applications. In her case, the best source of such courses turned out to be the local office of the company which manufactured the computer used by her company.

The hands-on classes took her roughly 13 weeks to complete and were geared to people like her who had not studied computer science in school but who used data processing equipment in the performance of their jobs. As you may have guessed by now, after completing this short yet practical program, this financial analyst could run circles around her competition! And she avoided taking costly, difficult, and time-consuming courses which were a mandatory part of the masters degree program she initially considered.

Is the Additional Degree the Real Key to Moving Ahead?

If I had received a dollar for every person who decided to go back for an extra sheepskin, only to discover that it did not open the doors it was supposed to have sprung open, I would be a very wealthy person. Our firm's experience has been, more often than not, that a person's ability to advance depends on other than academic credentials. Again and again we have discovered that your ability to make decisions, to communicate effectively orally and/or in writing, to listen, and so on are more important criteria for achieving success in a given field than a bachelor or masters degree. Given this fact, the two or three years spent at night pursuing the extra sheepskin could end up doing nothing more than adding to the frustration of the person who completed the requirements, and then saw nothing come of this effort.

THE THIRD CORNERSTONE AND LESS TRADITIONAL EDUCATION OPTIONS

Against this backdrop, the third cornerstone in your self-development strategy is really obvious: *Make sure each investment you make in yourself in order to improve your future chances for success is the most appropriate one for the personal development you identify.* Putting it another way, make sure your self-development program is strategic. If you are totally objective with regard to the competitive weakness you need to overcome or the competitive strength you need to build on and approach this need or opportunity directly, your self-improvement program should take less effort and less time and more importantly, be more likely to move you further ahead. In this regard, here are some less traditional educational options worth exploring:

Degrees by Mail from Accredited Institutions That Accept Life Experience in Lieu of Academic Courses

Most of these institutions are in California and are generally expensive for the amount of academic support they provide. On the other hand, since your life experience is accepted in place of certain courses, you can complete your degree far sooner and with a good deal less effort. (It is possible to earn a doctoral degree in under one year, for example.) The institutions offering such programs are fully approved by the State of California Department of Education. In fact, after contacting a number of these by-mail degree shops, I can offer only one caveat: the diplomas from such schools are not well received in academic circles so if you plan to teach, they are less appropriate for you than for the businessperson in search of credentials. How do you find such schools? They continually advertise in "in-flight" magazines. Among the better known ones: California Coastal University, Kensington University, and Beverly Hills University. If a quick yet honest sheepskin is all you desire, they may just be the answer.

Degrees That Require Little or No Time on Campus

Today, approximately 75 major, well-established universities including Purdue University, Penn State, and the University of Michigan offer about 1,000 extension courses by mail and 3 state colleges (New York State University in Albany, Illinois State University in Springfield, Ill., and Edison College in Trenton, N.J.) accept such courses in their nonresidential degree programs. You can write directly to these schools for more information or to *Guide to Independent Study,* National University Extension Program, Suite 350, One Dupont Circle, Washington, D.C. 20036. Keep in mind that these by-mail programs are not a breeze. The academic criteria for at-home students is as stringent as that for on-campus students. But they are far less costly and less demanding to you (and your career) than taking a leave of absence from work and returning to campus.

Multi-Week On-Campus Certificate Programs

The Advanced Management Program (AMP) at Harvard Business School, for example, is about ten weeks, but it is probably one of the best time investments any career person could make. This is true for several reasons: First, acceptance into the program is limited to persons with demonstrated management potential so that an AMP certificate is a well-known advancement credential among business leaders. Second, the program is specifically designed to provide such people with the perspective they need to function more successfully at higher levels in their organizations. Third, the program requires company sponsorship. As such, your application should alert senior-level people in your organization to your desire and commitment to growth in your organization. Fourth, the program enables you to exchange ideas with peers in other organizations. Hopefully, their experience should stimulate your capacity for providing more corporate benefits in your own company. Finally, an AMP program certificate entitles you to membership in the Harvard Business School Alumni Association, itself a valuable credential. If you doubt that at this point in your career you could get into the prestigious Harvard AMP program and question its discussion here, keep in mind that AMP programs are now offered at other major universities such as Dartmouth and Stanford and at lesser known colleges as well. (Such programs provide an excellent source of income to sponsoring institutions and an opportunity to utilize university facilities during summer months when buildings might otherwise remain empty.)

So if you contact business schools in your locale, you may just find a multi-week AMP-style certificate program not only in general management, but also in marketing, research, corporate finance, and so on. These programs are designed specifically for middle managers, and any could provide you with an additional credential and tie to another academic institution. (About the only drawback to such programs is that they are likely to separate you from your business and family for a few weeks, and since they are likely to occur in the summer, they could kill vacation plans.)

Internal Company Educational Programs

Many companies (e.g., G.E., DuPont, and Xerox) have formal instructional programs to help develop their own employees. Some of these programs are highly competitive, and you must apply for admission in them. (G.E.'s Manufacturing Management Program is one; it is considered by G.E. management to be equivalent to an M.B.A. although no degree is conferred.)

Alternately, other internally-provided instructional programs are less formal and include a variety of practical courses taught by company personnel or instructors from local colleges. You may elect to take such training on a one-by-one basis at your option.

Typically, employees are encouraged to take company-sponsored courses within their own discipline (e.g., engineering, accounting). But individuals can generally persuade bosses (or the training department) to permit their taking courses outside of their own disciplines, and we are familiar with many career people who expanded their knowledge, credentials, and horizons within their own companies by pursuing such interdisciplinary programs. An engineer, for example, with a background in technical purchasing and inventory control, believed his career progress was blocked as a result of his specialization. Over a four-year period, he completed eight internally given courses in manufacturing management. Armed with certificates of completion in these programs, he persuaded a senior manufacturing executive in his company to give him an opportunity in production supervision even though such interdisciplinary shifts occurred rarely in his company.

Obviously, internal company education programs are not available universally. If your company does not offer such programs, you might suggest that they consider giving them, or alternately, that they sponsor you at courses given by local colleges. Many companies pay for externally-provided courses when the company itself is not in a position to have its own staff conduct such programs. If you ask, you could be pleasantly surprised to find that your initiative was all that was needed to get this type of no-cost, highly visible self-development program going in your company and that you can take advanced courses in your field at no cost to you.

Intensive Seminars Which Teach Functional Skills

If your analysis of your competitive position suggests, for example, that you aren't as good a decision maker as you'd like to be, you might do well to take a seminar like the one given for the past two decades by Kepner-Tregoe out of Princeton, N.J. The nearly one million graduates of this program praise it highly for the practical formula it teaches to make decision making easier and better.

Most intensive seminars like this one take less than a week to complete. Still, if you are lacking in a basic functional skill, their impact on your career may be far greater than a degree that could take you years to earn.

The American Management Association publishes a catalog of literally hundreds of similar intensive seminars offered by the A.M.A. They range from finance for the non-financial executive to personnel selection and hiring. A.M.A. offers continuing education credits for its seminars (in some cases, these may be transferable for advanced degree credits by some colleges, an added plus.) Dun & Bradstreet and Fred Prior Seminars also offer a variety of intensive seminar programs. You'll find a comprehensive list of companies providing this type of intensive program in the annual directory issue of *Training* magazine in your local library.

One nice feature of this self-development tool is that the organizations that offer these seminars bring them to you. Most are offered in a half-dozen to dozen major cities so that your travel expense in connection with this type of learning experience is minimized, and with a number of dates to choose from, can easily be worked into your schedule.

Another peripheral benefit is that the cost of this type of functional skills program is often assumed by the company that sends its employees to it. If your appraisal of your competitive position suggests you lack a functional skill, it couldn't hurt to ask your boss if your company will sponsor your attendance at one. You may find that such programs cost you nothing and provide you with an opportunity to learn a great deal of practical information in minimal time.

There is only one caveat in suggesting that you pursue these intensive, functional self-development programs: while such training can give you enormous new insights into key skill areas, the concentrated nature of this type of training is likely to provide only a temporary spurt in your competence level. Unless you make a conscious effort to practice the techniques learned in such seminars rigorously and continuously after completing them, the potential of such learning can be wasted.

Franchised Personal Development Courses

Payne-Lendman's experience has convinced us that many careers stall not because of a functional skill deficiency (e.g., a lack of knowledge of how to use computers, how to hire people, and the like) but rather because of a low level of competence in the personal skills arena. You may, in fact, have worked with a peer whose personal deficiencies caused his or her career growth to fizzle—an engineer or M.B.A., perhaps, who obviously knew how to deal effectively with technical or business concepts (and who could provide corporate benefits as a result), but who, at the same time, was totally inadequate when it came to dealing with people, communicating ideas, demonstrating leadership, and so on (and thus incapable of providing the personal benefits necessary to advance his or her career). Fortunately, there are courses available that provide practical assistance to those who recognize that this area of self-development requires attention and who then make up their minds to do something about it.

Perhaps the best known of these franchised, personal development programs is the Dale Carnegie Course, which has been given for more than half a century. This program can help you become more aware of what motivates peers and mentors, how to apply this motivation to your working relationships with them, how to increase your level of self-confidence, how to communicate your ideas more effectively, and so on. From time to time, we have sent members of our own staff to the Dale Carnegie program to learn how to deal with one or several of these personal development areas, and the results have been outstanding.

Programs like the Dale Carnegie course generally require a commitment of only one evening a week plus a few additional hours during the week for reading and practice and take only three or four months to complete. They offer graduate certificates but are not considered in any way to be academic programs. Nonetheless, the $500 investment you might make in this type of program could be one of the best you'll ever make if personal rather than functional skills development is what is required to advance your career.

The Dale Carnegie program is by no means the only such personal growth program available to you. Courses in transactional analysis, interpersonal communications, time management, organizing work, speed reading, executive grooming, and others are given periodically in many cities, frequently by franchised training companies. If you don't see ads for them in your local paper, check your area school board. Often such courses are incorporated into adult education programs. Or check with the major motels in your area. The free, introductory lectures designed to promote this type of program are often held in centrally located Holiday Inns, Ramadas, and the like.

Are self-improvement programs like the Dale Carnegie course, Silva mind control, Evelyn Wood's Reading Dynamics, and others for you? It's hard to say. But our firm is convinced that three out of every four outplacements we do for performance reasons actually reflect weaknesses in personal rather than functional skills. Some career people find it difficult to own up to this fact when they are outplaced.

There is a simple way to determine if personal skills development is what is called for in your case. If you feel more than adequate technically in your position and yet are not moving as quickly as you think you should within your own organization, this type of program could be worth exploring. It could do more to increase chances of achieving your success potential than any formal functional or skills training you could pursue.

Industry-Sponsored Certification Programs

Recently there has been interest on the part of industry group members to strengthen the professionalism of practitioners in their particular fields. Thus, today, certified public accountants have been joined by chartered life underwriters, certified personnel consultants, certified security dealers, and so on. The difficulty of earning certification varies enormously within industry groups. While it could take years to earn a coveted C.P.A. (and many accountants fail to secure one), in other fields a few months of at-home study and a Saturday spent taking tests could earn you certification initials following your name.

If you are committed to pursuing a career in a particular field, and certification is provided by an industry group, the time and effort required to secure such certification may be far more valuable to you as a door opener than an advanced academic degree.

Convention Seminar Programs

Many organizations hold conventions. For some, these serve as an opportunity for social and business connections rather than for self-development. But the seminars offered at such conventions can be a fast, effective way to upgrade your skills and knowledge in your field. Such programs given at the Direct Mail Marketing Association's convention, for example, could make you more competent in list selection, mailing procedures, catalog production, and so on in just a few hours time. Seminars held as part of the American Society of Personnel Administrators could introduce you to new benefits, practices, and regulations, new selection processes, and others.

Thus, while the image of industry conventions is often that of a social affair, they do, in fact, provide exceptional opportunities to increase your skills base quickly and at little or no cost, provided you can get your company to sponsor you.

The nontraditional educational opportunities cited previously (and, perhaps, others like technical correspondence schools or adult education classes) could turn out to be more cost-effective self-development alternatives than the advanced degree so many career people doggedly pursue. Thus this suggestion: Be sure your educational decisions reflect the needs you hope such training can fulfill (e.g., a quick spurt in technical skills, a new credential that will improve your shelf image, a low-cost way to improve your personal benefits' ability).

NONACADEMIC SELF-DEVELOPMENT ALTERNATIVES

Interestingly enough, after analyzing goals and alternatives, a good many people come to the conclusion that no formal education program is called for! This is not to say that these people have no need for additional self-development. Not at all. Rather it's because these career professionals realize they have invested too much time and effort trying to advance their careers through educational pursuits when, in fact, nonacademic self-development alternatives might be more beneficial. Let's explore some.

Taking an Active Role in a Club or Industry Association

You might doubt that you could undertake a self-development program by joining a club. But many career professionals have done just that. Toastmasters International, for example, has helped many an introverted and/or self-conscious career person gain confidence and poise in front of groups, and this acquired skill has been a factor in his or her fulfillment of his or her potential. Kiwanis and the Jay Cees have been the leadership training ground for many successful executives.

We have in our own organization, for example, a high-ranking individual who has no college credentials. Yet his peers rank his judgment and persuasiveness among business executives as outstanding. This individual secured his higher education in Kiwanis; he observed how successful businesspeople conducted themselves in its committees and its general meetings and emulated them. And not only did it provide him with the sophistication he needed to perform better in his job, but it also gave him something else as well. This person has hanging on his wall a plaque of appreciation presented to him when he retired as president. That bronze plaque from Kiwanis is his equivalent of a college diploma—a credential of great importance to the advancement of his career.

Our employee is not the only person who has benefited from the learning power of clubs. We've witnessed major transformations in the confidence level of female career people who have been forced into leadership positions in Junior Leagues and Junior Woman's Clubs at a time when they were unable to gain this type of management training within the companies that employed them. Needless to say, these individuals later secured supervisory positions in their own companies but only after the assertive qualities they acquired as leaders within their clubs were manifested in their work environments.

Active membership in an industry association can be of even more value than membership in a club. The extra ingredient, of course, is the career-related focus of the association. The Tidewater chapter of the American Society of Personnel Administrators, for example, is an invaluable source of techniques for its members. Faithful monthly attendance could make any personnel director more knowledgeable when he or she returned to his or her organization. And the more active your participation, the more beneficial such membership could be to you. The current program chairman of the association confided to me, for example, that her position resulted in her researching areas that she had no reason to become exposed to in her job and meeting some experts in her field that she would never have had any dealings with through her company.

Writing Articles and Books

"If you want to become an expert, put your ideas between hard covers." There's a lot of truth to this. Literally hundreds of people have told me on first meeting that they had read one of my books and were honored to meet the author. In point of fact, the world bestows a special sort of prestige upon those whose names appear on the covers of books.

As such, publication has the capacity to enhance the image of any career person who has the discipline to set his or her own ideas down on paper. For the person who has not secured an advanced degree in a field where many of his or her competitors have, writing a book or an article appearing in a respected industry publication may be an even better alternative. It certainly should improve your resume and/or the write-up about you in your personnel folder. It could even lead to articles about you in your company's newspaper or magazine which would further enhance your prestige. Reviews of published material and interviews with authors could compound the honor that the original publication conveys.

Most importantly, the publication of your ideas gives them far more credence and authority than they would have were you to type them out and submit them to your boss. This enhanced image has resulted in authors being singled out for promotion within their own organizations and receiving unsolicited offers from other organizations on more than one occasion!

Naturally, the better received your book or article, the greater the prestige and authority it confers upon you. Quite obviously, too, the better known the publisher of your book or the better read the periodical in which your article appears, the greater the rewards of writing. (Thus, circulating your manuscript to better known publishers and publications first makes a good deal of sense.) But if you are turned down by your first publisher, don't stop sending your manuscript out. It is better to have been published by a lesser known outfit than not to have been published at all!

There is still one additional benefit in publishing that should be mentioned briefly here: Writing your thoughts down can be a valuable self-development experience even if what you write is never published. Writing can help you learn how to better organize and communicate your ideas. In our experience, many brilliant, creative business executives have stalled in their careers simply because they were unable to get across their technical competence to others.

If you are afraid to start writing, keep this thought in mind: Writing is a learned discipline like drawing, tennis, or bike riding. The more you do it, the easier it gets. If you have little opportunity for expressing your ideas on your job now, forcing yourself to write for a publisher or periodical can help you sharpen a skill which has the power to propel you ahead both inside and outside your present organization.

At this point, many readers—perhaps even you—may be thinking: "I've always had in my mind the idea for a book. Maybe I should start writing. But it takes an awful lot of work to write a book. What if no publisher accepts it?" This kind of thinking has led many a potential author to put away his or her pen. And rightly so.

The fact is, however, that you don't have to complete a 300-page manuscript in order to convince a publisher to put your ideas in print. Most writers (myself included) don't tackle a full manuscript until we have a commitment from a publisher. And the easiest and fastest way to get this is to write a sample chapter, the introduction to your book, which explains its purpose and intent, and a short synopsis of the rest of the chapters you propose to write. With this approach, you minimize your effort prior to sourcing a publisher.

Don't overlook trade magazines—particularly the smaller ones—as potential outlets for your writing. Many such magazines are almost desperate for good, relevant material in their fields. And the smaller magazines often operate on very limited budgets. If you are willing to publish for little or no fee, forward an interestingly written article to one of the magazines in your field. Your chances of getting yourself in print may be better than you had imagined! And once you've been in print somewhere, it's easier to find others who will publish you. It's worth a try.

Giving Speeches

Speaking to an industry association or company organization offers much the same image-building benefits as publishing. And, the more august the group you speak to, the more you enhance your reputation as an authority in your field. If you are one of those people who enjoys talking but is apprehensive about writing an article or book, the speakers' circuit could be an excellent self-development alternative. In fact, we frequently come across resumes which incorporate a separate section describing the groups a particular executive has addressed and the topics he or she has talked about. Summaries alluding to speeches before national and regional industry conventions can be most impressive! But talks to local chapters of industry-recognized groups within your field and/or related fields can be meaningful, too. And these local chapters are frequently desperate for speakers.

As such, you don't have to be a renowned authority in order to secure a speaking engagement. If you have completed some interesting research in your field, worked with an interesting or well-known person, or been involved in a project with news value, you have a very good chance of selling a program chairman on an invitation to talk to his or her group.

Finding groups to talk to may be easier than you might have imagined. The *Encyclopedia of Associations*, published by Gale Research and available in many libraries, can provide you with data on every national association in your field. A phone call to the national headquarters should reveal the local chapter officers to write or call. You might also consider contacting the local chamber of commerce, Kiwanis, and other civic and church groups, provided you are able to gear your material to more general interest meetings. Obviously, talking to such audiences is less prestigious than talking to groups within your field. But, as one of our clients put it: "Most people looking over your resume assume that Kiwanis invited you rather than that you went to them. That can look pretty good on the record!" It goes without saying that finding a local group interested in having you talk to them will require some effort. But, if what you have to say is informative and interesting, it will be easier to attract additional audiences once you have proven yourself as an effective speaker.

And keep this in mind: if the field you are in is itself newsworthy, you may be able to locate a speakers' bureau interested in arranging speaking engagements for you. Such organizations generally prefer to promote well-known speakers, but if your topic is of significant interest, it couldn't hurt to contact such an organization. They advertise for potential speakers in *Advertising Age* occasionally and in the in-flight magazines as well.

If you are not up to speaking engagements, you might try to become a member of a discussion group representing a professional or an industry organization. Remember, the program chairperson's job is not an easy one; finding appropriate panel members is usually a chore. So a call from you could lead to an invitation to become a panelist. This could also enhance your reputation in your field.

The secret of building your image through speeches and/or panel presentations is to go after speaking opportunities. If you wait to be invited, you may never have the occasion! If this type of self-development strategy makes sense for you, a little campaigning could really pay off.

Teaching at a Local University, College, or Technical School

If you are skilled in a particular field such as marketing or engineering or in a particular function required in your field such as copywriting or programming, you might do well to consider seeking a position as an adjunct faculty member at a local teaching institution, particularly if it has a good reputation in academia or the business world.

Finding a position as an adjunct faculty member may also be easier than you think. The pay for teaching continuing education courses is generally a pittance (e.g., one of our staff serves on the evening school faculty of a local college and receives $10 per 2-hour class taught!). So the turnover is often high. What's more, adjunct faculty generally have day-time positions in industry and teach for the fun of it at night. As such, out-of-town trips and business commitments can interfere with individual classes. Thus, you may find you can work your way into a teaching position just by registering as a substitute teacher for a course that is already being taught by someone else. Business-related relocations lead to faculty resignations, too, so that putting your name on file with the evening division of a local college could lead to future teaching assignments.

And don't overlook opportunities to teach courses given by your company if it has its own continuing education program. Within your own organization, being a faculty member carries with it the prestige and authority that being an adjunct faculty member at a college carries outside.

Interestingly enough, a part-time teaching assignment can do more than just provide you with an additional credential to market. You may find that teaching sharpens your ability to train subordinates (a corporate benefit) and your ability to organize material within your field. There are other benefits, too: the platform skills you develop as an instructor may make you a better presenter to management.

You may even find yourself learning as you teach, particularly if you are following a lesson plan that requires you to instruct in areas that you do not deal with everyday. If you are lucky, your students may even keep you current on developments in your field, particularly if they work for other companies in your industry during the day.

Finally, when you hold a teaching assignment, it provides a means of communicating to your bosses and mentors that you not only have the ability to do your own job but also to teach others to do it. This opportunity to demonstrate that you have the capacity to instruct people could help you get a chance to train subordinates at work if you don't do so now.

Seeing a Psychologist

Many people we outplace lost their jobs because they were unable to deal effectively with their bosses. In some cases, the relationships which these outplaced people have with bosses mirror relationships they had with a parent many years before! Without realizing it, these outplaced persons use patterns developed in childhood to deal with people at work. Such patterns aren't usually appropriate. In cases like this, half a dozen sessions with a good behavioral psychologist can do more to help these people advance in their careers than a dozen extra degrees.

Do you really need to see a psychologist in order to unstall your career? Probably not. Our firm suggests that outplaced persons seek professional help in less than one in ten cases. But if you aren't sure why you don't please your bosses when you try to do so, consider this possibility. You just may need to better understand your own actions and reactions in your dealings with superiors. Don't be embarrassed to at least consider this self-development tool. You won't be the first career person to benefit from such counselling.

For a listing of psychologists who might help, check to see if your local library has the *American Psychological Association–Directory*. It lists 54,000 members geographically. If your library doesn't have a copy, call the Association headquarters (202-833-7600). They'll give you the names of psychologists in your community.

Contact an Image Consultant

After reading Chapters 5 and 7, you're likely to have little doubt as to the importance of your image in successfully marketing your talents. Experience has shown that it is virtually impossible for you—or any career person—to achieve your full potential if your bosses and mentors do not believe you have the image required for future growth. It is likewise practically impossible to move ahead in any organization unless your shelf impression is consistent with the one which your bosses and or mentors favor.

For most readers, an in-depth review of Chapter 5 will enable you to develop a fairly accurate portrait of your present image. Similarly, reviewing Chapter 7 will enable you to determine just how appropriate your image is vis-à-vis the key buyers in your success market. At this point, even if you have never considered your image as a factor in your success before, you should have a pretty good idea of what you need to do in order to enhance your shelf impression.

Quite obviously, some aspects of your image can't be changed. You can't very well grow six inches, for example, just because you know you lack psychological weight. On the other hand, if your image could be improved by weight loss or gain, a different hair style, new attire or accessories, the development of different speech patterns, and the like, most readers will be capable of establishing an appropriate image-improvement program on their own.

If you need help, however, in developing an accurate picture of your current image, or desire assistance in purchasing a wardrobe that will establish a more positive shelf impression for yourself, you'll be glad to know help is available to you. The most recent *Directory of Personal Image Consultants* (Editorial Service Company, N.Y.) lists more than 60 firms nationally which specialize in assisting middle and senior level executives to develop new, more positive shelf impressions. Such help is not inexpensive; you might expect to pay $500 to $5,000 for such aid. But if you sincerely believe your image may hinder you in your benefits delivery and can afford to invest in this element of your personal marketing campaign, you might want to consider professional counsel in this area.

One of the most valuable aspects of working with an image consultant is the televised interview of yourself which virtually all such image consultants provide. During the critique you'll see yourself in action. And it might prove to be an eye-opener, particularly if your speech patterns and listening habits are tarnishing an otherwise positive image. In all our high-level outplacements, and in every image development program our firm conducts, we videotape our clients. Quite frankly, many are shocked (and sometimes dismayed) at how they project on camera.

Fortunately, when most career people are made aware of how they come across as a result of videotaped interviews, they are most eager to begin programs to counter the negative aspects of the way they project. And following a few coaching sessions, there is usually a world of difference! This is particularly true for a client whose image had been adversely affected by awkward speech patterns, gestures, body English, and use of ungrammatical phrases. For those clients who project a defensive image on the T.V. screen or an uncaring attitude towards the interviewer, however, it is our experience that a psychologist is far more likely to succeed in changing the person's image than is a career consultant.

If you feel you need help in this area, get the image consultants directory. One caution: if you contemplate calling our firm for this type of help, please keep in mind that we work only for client companies. When we are asked to take on an image development project, it is usually for an executive "on the move," and the client company foots the bill.

Pursuing a New Job Opportunity

This book is all about how you can avoid looking for jobs by getting them to come to you. Nonetheless, there are occasions when you may need to bite the bullet and seek job alternatives now which will create future career opportunities for you inside or outside your company.

If, for example, you conclude that state-of-the-art technology is to be found only outside your department or company, you may elect to develop your technical competence by working for an organization capable of providing more or better tutelage. If you do elect to look elsewhere, be very careful to ensure that the technology you can learn is saleable later on. If you don't, a move can be a costly mistake.

Ted Bailey, for example, left one mainframe computer company for broadening at another mainframe company. He might just as easily have pursued opportunities in a minicomputer company. A few years later Ted confided to one of our counselors that he was sorry that he had not given greater thought to the direction of the data processing industry when he changed jobs since he could have earned a good deal more money had he joined a different company.

If you do elect to look elsewhere, think seriously also about the prestige of the company you are joining. Remember, just as in your personal life, people are known by the company they keep. If the outfit you hook up with isn't known or respected, your new back label may be tarnished, making it more difficult for you to pursue career advancement than if you had not moved from your present company.

Be careful, too, about the title you accept. Many people our firm has worked with have said to themselves that titles mean nothing and then used this rationale to accept positions less impressive than the ones they formerly held—just in order to join firms in which they thought they could learn more. The fact is that titles do mean a lot. And if you sacrifice title for training, your back label and shelf image could be adversely affected by your decision. In this case, your career may be stymied despite the fact that you are capable of delivering more or better corporate benefits as a result of the training you receive in your new affiliation.

If you are considering exploration of other job opportunities in order to enhance your functional knowledge, be sure also that such knowledge is really what is needed in order to advance your career. All too often individuals tell us they are technically stranded in their jobs (e.g., "There's no opportunity for growth for a person with my discipline.") when in reality their growth is blocked for nontechnical reasons. Thus, the fourth and final cornerstone in self-development programs is this: *Career progress is often more dependent on shelf image and personal benefits capability than it is on corporate benefits capacity or credentials. Be objective about your ability to please people and your projected image with bosses and mentors before you seek a new affiliation, an additional degree, or a new technical or functional skill. It may pay for you to work on your skill in delivering personal benefits and on enhancing the image you project first.* These could be the key to your future success.

REASONS FOR FAILURE
TO REALIZE FULL POTENTIAL

Given the enormous variety of self-improvement opportunities, academic and otherwise, it is difficult to understand how some career people explain away their failure to achieve their full potential with statements like "The competition was too tough in my field," or "Some of my peers had advantages over me." But we hear this kind of explanation from many of the people we outplace. In our judgment, career people who find themselves at a competitive disadvantage don't do so for lack of self-development opportunities. Rather, it is for other reasons:

• *They don't realize that they are not competitive until it's too late.* Then they discover to their surprise that others, particularly more recent graduates, have greater or more current knowledge than they or better credentials than they. This kind of painful discovery can be avoided, of course, if you evaluate your competitive position each year. So many people routinely take a physical each year; so few do a checkup on how well their back label, image, and ability to provide benefits compare to obvious and not so obvious competition in their fields.

• *When they do discover they are less than competitive, they decide it is impossible to do anything about it.* More often than not, they believe this because they have decided for themselves that they can only catch up with an additional degree. They realize this will take a year or more, and so they assume they'll always be behind competition. Hopefully, this chapter has suggested alternative sources of credentials and skills that can provide you with the competitive advantages you need to catch up to, and get ahead of, competition sooner.

• *They assume they are not doing as well as their peers for the wrong reasons.* All too often outplaced persons tell us that others with whom they compete outmaneuvered them because they had greater technical skill, better credentials, and so forth, when in point of fact, it was because the individuals we worked with lacked leadership or organizational skills or the ability to deal effectively with people.

It is not easy to be objective in assessing your competitive position and the reasons for it. Unless you are capable of honestly assessing your situation or solicit an objective appraisal of it from bosses or peers, you are likely to try to improve yourself in the wrong areas.

• *They decide at some point in their careers that self-improvement is simply not worth the effort.* Recently I heard the controller of a well-known company tell us that he'd sooner leave his company than have to go back to school. That's a reasonable personal decision. Generally speaking, younger career people are more eager to upgrade their competitive position than older ones because they see the investment in themselves as more likely to pay off. But if you analyze the people who have achieved the greatest successes in your field, you'll conclude that they steadfastly committed themselves to being a step ahead of competition. And so, they not only assessed their competitive situations honestly and regularly, but they also did what was necessary to improve their credentials, image, and skills. Only you can decide if achieving all the potential that is within you is worth the effort required to bring it out.

IMPROVING YOUR CHANCES...

1. Outside of growing on your job, do you have an ongoing program to upgrade yourself in the success market?

2. If a genie gave you one wish that would allow you to become more competitive, better in some way, in what area would you improve?

3. If you believe that you could improve your chances in your success market if you had more education, better credentials, better understanding of people, and the like, what have been the primary obstacles holding you back from your self-development program?

4. Are these obstacles insurmountable? What can you do about them?

5. How long would it take you to earn an additional degree related to your field? Would this extra credential help you to grow in your current area of endeavor?

6. In your case, how important is the source of the degree?

7. Are there industry groups with local chapters in your area? Could you upgrade your skills and knowledge by joining such groups?

8. When is the last time you attended a seminar related to your field? Do you attend more or less than others in your organization with whom you compete?

9. If you were to write a book or article in order to add to your credentials, what would it be about? Do you have enough background now to write this? Should you be developing data at this time?

10. Has your career progress stalled at any time? If it has, what would you honestly say were the primary reasons this occurred? Lack of degree? Credentials? Personal skills (speaking, writing, etc.)? People skills (ability to motivate, convince, lead, etc.)? Something else?

11. Have you ever had a friend who participated in a Dale Carnegie, Transactional Analysis, or similar personal development program? What was his or her reaction? Why do you think this person decided to take this program? Could you see the benefits to this person following the course?

12. If you were to change jobs today for the purpose of joining an organization that would help you grow in your field, which company (or companies) would you most want to join? Why? If it is unlikely that you could secure a job with such a company, what other options do you have to obtain the personal self-development that might have available to you in this company?

chapter nine

A strategy for developing new buyers of your talents

If you are familiar with Coast soap, you know it's not a major break-through in personal cleansing. Coast's marbelized coloring is very much akin to that of Irish Spring, a soap preceding it to market by several years. Coast's deodorant formula is a takeoff on Dial's, a personal cleansing bar that's been around for twenty-five years. Likewise, Coast's high-bubble formula is akin to Zest; its pleasantly fresh scent very similar to several other competitive products.

Yet Coast zoomed its way from obscurity to becoming one of the biggest selling toilet soaps in the U.S. in a matter of months. What was Coast's secret? For one thing, Procter & Gamble put all its selling muscle behind Coast and secured distribution for it in virtually every major food outlet in the country within a matter of weeks. But availability alone wasn't enough to make Coast a superstar in its category. Without buyers to take Coast off the shelf, it soon would have lost its position on the shelf.

Two other things made Coast enormously successful in spite of its not being a significantly better product than those already available. They are consumer awareness and consumer trial. Procter & Gamble invested millions and millions of dollars to announce Coast's introduction to the American public. At the time of its launching, it was nearly impossible to watch a half hour of T.V. without seeing the "eye opener" commercials supporting Coast's introduction. Likewise, the pages of home and women's magazines echoed Coast's name. During its introduction, Coast's message reached into 95% of U.S. households and reached the average viewer more than a dozen times during any four-week period. (Some heavy T.V. viewers probably were exposed to the Coast message more than 100 times during the first month or so after its launch.) So consumers were totally familiar with the Coast brand name and package by the time they went to the store.

The incredible pressure of advertising wasn't Coast's only source of consumer familiarity. Millions of bars of Coast Soap were mailed directly to U.S. households, enabling every member of these families to see it, feel it, and try it without spending a penny to do so. Within a matter of months, P&G developed such enormous awareness for Coast that it had become a household word!

The advertising and promotional pressure behind Coast is by no means unique. Major marketers in every packaged goods category realize that to sell their wares, they have to secure buyer familiarity (and, hence, initial sales) rapidly; it's one of the keys to every successful new product launch. As was pointed out in Chapter 7, familiarity is a major factor in buying decisions involving people within most companies, too. You'll recall that it has influenced many bosses' decisions on whom to promote.

AWARENESS AND TRIAL IN PERSONAL MARKETING

Not surprisingly, the first secret to being sought after by new buyers (i.e., people in companies other than your own) is also familiarity. If you want potential bosses and mentors in competitive organizations and in other industries to seek you out, you have to do something both to make sure that they know you exist and to make sure that they feel comfortable about you so that asking you to come to work for them is an easy decision. In sum, to secure new buyers for your talents, your strategy should be to create awareness of you among these buyers, and to provide them with some form of trial device. In this way not only your name is known to them, but you also are personally known to them.

Interestingly enough, this awareness/trial formula is exactly what you—and almost every career person—utilize each time you decide to change jobs and conduct a typical job search campaign. In a period of a few months, you try to get your name known to companies far and wide by sending your resume out to executive recruiters, employment agencies, and friends who in turn try to create awareness of you with talent buyers within companies in which your intermediaries have contacts. Hopefully, your campaign to create awareness of you among potential buyers of your talents pays off. If it does, you are invited in to interviews. When you sit down to talk with prospective employers, you then provide these potential buyers with a one to two hour opportunity to see what you might be like if they dealt with you every day on the job. Certainly, during your interview, you have a chance to review your credentials and experience. But in most cases, your interview is far more valuable to prospective employers because it gives them a trial size sample of you so that your potential employer can see for him- or herself what it would be like to work with you day in and day out.

As suggested in Chapter 2, there's an inherent weakness in this traditional approach to getting a new job and that's this: your effort to make potential buyers aware of you is concentrated into a very, very short time frame, and during the three or four month period in which you are looking for a new position, only a few potential buyers are likely to have an immediate need for your talents.

This book therefore proposes an alternative to the traditional "into-and-out-of-the-job-market" approach to finding buyers for your talents. That, of course, is to make a concerted, disciplined effort every day to create more and more awareness of you among as many probable buyers of your talents as you can possibly reach and to provide these buyers with an opportunity to sample you on an ongoing basis.

It goes without saying that this nontraditional approach is likely to lead to job offers more frequently than the traditional approach to getting a new job. These job offers could occur when you least expect them. Perhaps this concerns you. If it does, keep in mind that you don't have to accept any job offer just because it's tendered to you. And offsetting this concern should be the fact that if you create awareness of you among prospective buyers on a routine basis, you are far more likely to yield more and better job offers—one or more of which may well be worth leaving your present employer for!

CREATING AWARENESS AND TRIAL
AMONG POTENTIAL BUYERS
OF YOUR BENEFITS

When it comes to creating awareness and trial, there are two significant differences between a personal marketing campaign versus one for packaged goods brands. First, you can't very well spend millions of dollars on T.V. and magazines to promote awareness of the benefits you might offer to prospective employers! Similarly, there is no practical way to clone yourself so that you can provide thousands of potential employers with samples of you in action. It stands to reason, therefore, that the process of creating broad awareness of you will be a far slower one than for a branded item, and that, once you have made yourself known to a prospective buyer, you'll have to work at sustaining awareness of you over a long period of time. (Many a career person conducting a traditional job search has told us that they found their latest job by recontacting someone whom they had met many years before.) Thus, if you are to make a day-to-day awareness campaign work effectively to bring you job offers, you'll need to be cognizant of maintaining awareness of you among potential employers as well.

Fortunately, it is possible for any career person to both create and sustain awareness among many potential buyers of his or her talents without investing thousands of dollars in advertising or sampling. There are many avenues you can pursue. Following are some examples.

Writing Books and Speeches

Not only will putting your name in print enhance your image in your field, but it could also lead to greater awareness of you. So, if you elect to build your reputation through articles or books, here are two thoughts: First, be sure to let your readers know how to reach you, either by describing your present job in the text or by making sure the publisher does so in the credits. If you do, your writing may benefit you both by enhancing your image and by creating awareness of you.

If you doubt the power of print as a promotional medium to sell your talents, phone the editor of one or two trade periodicals in your field and find out what they pay for articles. (It's generally a token payment because the authors know the immense value of exposure of their names to colleagues.) Then contact some of the people whose names appear in these periodicals regularly as contributors. You'll be even more convinced! As an example, I once asked Dick Neff what prompted him to write a regular feature in *Ad Age* for many years. His answer: "It was the best source of contacts in the business." If you check, you'll find it is the best lead source in your business as well.

Joining Industry or Professional Clubs and Attending Industry Conventions

As was the previous case with writing, participating in industry-related groups can not only increase your knowledge and capacity to provide benefits within your existing organization, but it can also serve as a conduit to other organizations as well. In fact, industry groups and meetings may well be a more effective opportunity source than getting your name in print since active membership provides you with an opportunity to sample the whole you (your involvement, your effort, your social skills, your loyalty to the organization, and so on) and not just your ability to write.

I know a number of individuals who have changed jobs four or five times, on average, during their careers and who have never looked for a job! In each case they had job offers thrust upon them by close associates in the business organizations to which they belonged. When you ask these people how they happened to be offered jobs by fellow members of the business organizations they belonged to, the answer is usually the same: get to meetings early, make it your business to talk to members before the regular meetings begin, attend regularly, volunteer for assignments that involve working day to day with a few other members, and most importantly, socialize. Invite potential key persons out to have a drink or coffee after the meetings. Stay a day longer at conventions, make dates for meals with people you would like to know better, and so on. In sum, get to know as many people in your field as you can through such organizations and sample yourself—the whole you—whenever you can create a legitimate opportunity to do so.

It's possible that participation in an industry or professional society appeals to you, but you have not pursued this type of activity because there are no such organizations in your area.

If this is the case, form your own association! Recently I had the good fortune to speak to a one-year-old group of human resource managers. (Their titles varied from compensation specialist to Vice-President of Personnel.) The person who organized the club was none other than the program Vice-President with whom I sat at the head table.

During this luncheon he told me both how and why he had made this organizing effort. Let me share his reasons with you. After moving to a fairly remote part of New Jersey and discovering he had no contact with people in his field, he went to the local chamber of commerce and suggested a subsidiary organization made up of people with backgrounds similar to his own. With the chamber's financial backing and prestige, he then contacted all companies in the area and solicited members. His reason for doing this was not just intellectual stimulation from his peers. He confided in me that his family did not want to move again, and he had no networking source. As a result of forming the club, he now has sampled his organizational skills to more than 70 association members who meet regularly once each month.

This case history is not singular; if you want to make yourself known to persons outside your company who can influence your career but have no active source to reach them, create your own. It obviously can be done, and it can be worth it.

Teaching and Learning

When you think about it, there's a lot more to be gained in the classroom than an education. Whether you are conducting the class to add to your teaching credentials or taking a class to add to your knowledge, you expose yourself regularly to potential sources of career assistance.

If you are the one giving a class, you can easily capitalize on these sources by asking everyone to describe their backgrounds at the beginning of the semester. Then, cultivate friendships with those students in your field or profession at similar or higher levels in their organizations.

If you are a student, you can do the same thing although it may not be as easy if the instructor does not have each student introduce him- or herself to the class. What you need to do in this case is to make a concerted effort to introduce yourself to each of your classmates during the course. Then, make it your business to find a way to stay in touch with them after the course is over. One obvious way is to ask the teacher if you can create a roster of classmates by circulating a name-and-address list in class, which you'll type and copy for distribution.

And don't neglect developing a friendship with your instructor. The person teaching a continuing education course in your field must have a professional background in this area. Regardless of your grade, instructors can help you long after you have completed the course *if* you get to know them during the course. Witness the case of the young woman who took a class in editorial writing given by a writer named Clay Felker, the person who went on to become editor of the *New York Post* and *New York* magazine. Before she had completed the program, the young woman had secured from her instructor a list of his close associates in the field, and by personally contacting each of them, secured an associate editor position for herself! But that wasn't all. She got back to each of Felker's associates and let them know where she was and annually updated them on how she was doing. The result of this planned awareness campaign was that several years later one of these contacts hired her into a senior editorial position.

Developing Friendships With Sellers and Buyers

If you have occasion to buy from a supplier, even if it's rarely and even if the items you purchase are of little value, get to know your supplier personally. If you doubt the value of developing friendships with the peddlers in your field, consider the case of Kirk, a pension fund administrator whom our firm outplaced about eight weeks ago. Kirk had been with our client company only nine months, and things hadn't worked out. Our client generously gave Kirk a ten-week severance. Kirk was panicked beyond belief, feeling that he would never secure a position during this short period in view of poor economic conditions and considering the fact that he simply was not a social person. Fortunately, Kirk worked daily with a number of institutional stockbrokers on his job, and as part of the outplacement process, we suggested a number of techniques to use in contacting them. Within six weeks Kirk had a new job paying $10,000 more than he had previously made. What happened was that these brokers not only supplied Kirk with more than 40 contacts to pursue, but they also actually unearthed eight currently unfilled positions that Kirk was qualified for!

Thus, through suppliers, Kirk developed not one, but two offers within 40 days, and neither had been advertised or given to an executive recruiter! Such is the pull of suppliers who are anxious to please a past buyer who could become an even more appreciative buyer in future.

When I reviewed the alternative job offers with Kirk, he confided to me that during the nine months he was working for our client's company and wasn't looking, his broker suppliers had advised him of an additional three offers that he had not bothered to explore. The potential awareness value of suppliers is so great that even if you no longer buy from a supplier, it pays to stay in touch. The person who sold to you at one time in the past may well expect you to be in a position to buy from him or her again. Thus, they have a strong motive for exposing your name and talents to other clients who may need someone like you even if you're not now buying from them.

If your job involves selling to clients rather than buying from vendors, you have a potent source for exposing your talents outside of your own company, too. Obviously, buyers have less motivation and opportunity to expose your name and background to persons who could use your talent than do vendors who sell to you. Even so, they can be of great value to your career if you get to know them on a personal basis. The reason is simple: you may not secure as much awareness through this source as from suppliers, but every time you call on a prospect or buyer, you have an opportunity to demonstrate yourself in a business situation. This sampling of your talents can pay off in unsolicited job offers.

Some real-life examples: a college-educated young woman who worked as a hostess at a restaurant was offered a career position in a public relations firm by the principal who was very impressed with the way she dealt with the public. An account executive at Norman, Craig, and Kummel, an ad agency, was offered a position as a brand manager at Chesebrough-Pond's, the client he called upon. In this new position, the former account executive earned 25% more the day he joined! And we know of many senior auditors with public accounting firms who have been asked to join client companies in the capacity of controller, treasurer, and in one case, chief financial officer, because key people in these companies were so impressed with these individuals they sampled during the tax season.

The fact is, however, that many people call on customers for years without really getting to know them personally. Consequently, they neither learn of ways in which they can provide personal or significant corporate benefits to their clients and prospects nor do these potential employers learn that the salespeople who call on them are interested in pursuing other career alternatives. Buyers of products or services your company sells are obvious buyers of you as well. Not to cultivate opportunities to sample the whole you is to overlook a buyer already aware of your name. This is unfortunate.

Conducting Legitimate Intra-industry Business

Contacting your competitors is not illegal except for price fixing. And there are good reasons to get in touch with your counterparts within companies in your industry. For example, personnel directors in one company could benefit enormously from contact with personnel directors in another company for the purpose of discussing approaches to common safety problems, methods of complying with E.E.O. guidelines, new kinds of benefits programs, flexible hours, two-career families, and so on. Similarly, marketing people could benefit from contacting marketing people in other companies making products complementary to their own for the purpose of discussing joint "bread and butter" promotions, co-op advertising, and other ideas. Production people could benefit from meeting with competitors who have purchased automated equipment they are considering purchasing, and so on.

The reasons for interaction between persons of similar backgrounds in competitive firms, both large and small, are many. But the fact is that only a small percent of individuals with reason to interact with competitors make a concerted effort to do so. If you include yourself in that large group that could legitimately contact other companies in your industry, but has not consistently and aggressively done so, you are missing out on a valuable opportunity to create awareness of you by the most likely future buyers of your talents! This could be a costly mistake, particularly if you work in a small, tightly-knit industry.

How do you get in touch with competitors? By creating legitimate opportunities for mutual contact. Examples of this include: starting an industry association in your area, developing a local committee to discuss new quality standards, establishing an industry certification program if none exists in your industry, and developing a system for sharing materials that could be in short supply. Contacting potential employers long *before* you consider changing companies has obvious advantages. Don't be afraid to pursue this underutilized personal marketing opportunity.

Participating in Intercompany Sports Programs

Playing league softball is unique. Your job title doesn't matter; no one really cares if you are a vice-president or an office boy. If you can hit the ball and field a difficult catch, that's all that counts. The equalizing factor of sports organizations makes them particularly attractive as a way of developing awareness of you outside the company with more senior people who you couldn't possibly get to know otherwise.

Obviously, some sports are likely to put you in contact with more valuable potential mentors than others. If you are lucky enough to be included in a foursome at a very private golf club or play a round-robin match at the local tennis club, for example, your chances of rubbing elbows with people who may be in positions to hire people of your background are greater than, say, participating in a bowling league. But *any* sports league carries with it the opportunity of meeting people further along with their careers than you and who could be potential bosses!

Importantly, sports provide a unique opportunity to sample your best personal qualities. You can demonstrate, for example, your competitiveness, your will to win, your ability to remain cool under fire, your team-orientation, and so on. And you can do this in a matter of an hour or so while you are on the playing field! A sports league may also provide you with an opportunity to deliver a personal benefit to a potential boss. If you are capable of helping someone in your industry improve his or her game by offering helpful suggestions as you play—or even by just giving this person someone to practice with—you may create a residue of goodwill that may well transcend the corporate benefits you could provide for the organization that this person works for. It is not at all surprising for us to hear the outplaced persons we work with describe how their sports contacts resulted in job offers.

Interestingly enough, even if you are not a player, sports can have an impact on the awareness of you among your counterparts in other companies. If you are an avid sports fan, your ability to talk the game with a potential boss or mentor during a break at an industry association meeting could create a special bond between you. Similarly, coaching youth sports could bring you into contact with people who could become key figures in your professional life. As a case in point, one person our firm worked with told us that his coaching Little League was the prime factor in his being hired into his present position! It seems that the father of one of the boys on his team was president of the company he later joined. You couldn't ask for a better introduction! If you enjoy sports—playing, talking, coaching—take advantage of this fact regularly to both expose yourself to growth opportunities and to sample the personal qualities you might offer if an opportunity were thrust upon you.

Talking to Strangers

If you think back, you'll likely recall that as a child you were told not to talk to strangers. And if you are like most people, this advice still lingers in your mind as you sit in crowded airports, on planes, in hotel lobbies, and so on. It obviously takes effort to start a conversation with someone you don't know, but as long as the person next to you appears presentable, it could well be worth retraining yourself to do just this. Ernie Lendman, chairman of Lendman Associates, the largest producer of job fairs in the U.S. (a company with which we are affiliated), makes it a point to introduce himself to businesspeople he meets in his extensive travels. Ernie invariably returns with business cards of potential clients who have firsthand knowledge of his company and a most pleasant sampling of him personally. Ernie Lendman's ability to turn strangers into friends is exceptional, but it could happen to anyone who tries to do this. One of our recent outplacement clients who flew from his home in Syracuse to work with one of our counsellors in Virginia Beach advised the counsellor on his arrival that he sat next to an individual in his own field who, before the plane landed, had given him the names of three of his friends in executive positions in companies that our client had planned to pursue!

How can you get into a conversation with a complete stranger? If you see the person next to you reading a trade periodical in your field, it's easy. But if the person next to you is staring out into space, then what can you do? One tested opener is to ask your companion if he or she is travelling to the plane's next destination or beyond. No matter what the reply, you then ask if he or she is from the actual destination city. This can naturally lead to a question on the purpose of the trip, which can then lead to an inquiry about the person's profession or business. From that point on, just ask genuinely interested questions about what this person's job is in his or her company. And you are home free!

Is it worth talking to strangers this way? Unless you have pressing business matters in your briefcase, yes. It is a rare opportunity both to make other career people aware of you and to demonstrate your friendly, outgoing style. By the time you exchange business cards, you may have created a business relationship that could be a key source of assistance later in your career.

CREATING AWARENESS AND TRIAL
OF YOUR BENEFITS
WITHIN YOUR ORGANIZATION

At this point you might be asking yourself this legitimate question: "Supposing I have no intention whatsoever of leaving my company at any time, does it make sense to go to all this trouble to get my name known to people outside my company?" The record would indicate that the answer is still "Yes," and for several reasons. In the first place, one never knows when someone outside his or her company might approach with an opportunity that is simply too good to turn down. Now it stands to reason that if no one outside your company knows about you, the chances of this happening are infinitely smaller than if your talents are known beyond the corporate doors. Why prevent this golden opportunity from coming to you by remaining anonymous to the outside world?

In the second place, you may just find that being offered a golden opportunity *outside* your company does wonders for your career *inside* your own organization. Nothing makes an object so valuable as two persons bidding on it. The same holds true in personal marketing. Many a client of our firm has faced critical career choices during his or her career that involved staying with a company or accepting a position with another firm. And often the companies these persons were with offered internal advancement opportunities to the individuals concerned only when confronted with the possibility of losing them.

For the moment, let's accept as fact that you won't leave your present employer under any circumstances. Then your goal must be to maximize exposure of your name and talents inside your own organization. There are several ways to create awareness and trial internally that are worth pursuing. These include:

Dining Strategically

If you're like most career people, it is more than likely that you rou-tinely eat lunch with a group of people you work closely with. If you do, you are probably missing out on opportunities to know others in your organization better than you now do. As a case in point, Noel, a financial analyst in a health-and-beauty aids company, systematically made lunch dates with people in other departments with whom he occasionally worked in the performance of his own job. Not only did these once casual business associates appreciate the time Noel took to get to know them better, but they got to know Noel better and came to realize qualities about Noel which were easily overlooked in infrequent and strictly busi-ness meetings. As you might expect, one of the people Noel got to know well as a result of his lunch invitations was a group brand manager who invited Noel to join the brand management department. An interdepart-ment transfer had never occurred before at this company, and it became the single most significant turning point in Noel's career as he himself went on to become a V.P. and director of brand management! Case histories like this don't happen every day. But the point is they *do* happen. And, in every instance, it's because you made it your business to make them happen.

Your chances of getting to know and be known by potential men-tors and sponsors are particularly good if your company has an executive dining room or other exempt-employee dining facility. The secret of making the company dining rooms a part of your personal marketing plan is to systematically make it your business to eat with people you don't regularly work with.

How can you do this without seeming to slight members of your own department? Just by being honest and telling them that once or twice a week you like to dine with people you don't know so you can get to know more people in your company. There's nothing wrong with this, and your peers will probably respect you for it.

In sum, you can't create awareness by clinging tenaciously to asso-ciates you already know. Make it your business, therefore, to better know more people within your organization; you never know when such easily made associations can really pay off!

Joining Interdepartmental Groups Within Your Company

Volunteering to represent a department on your company's United Way or Blood Bank campaign committees may seem like an unnecessary waste of energy. But the payoff to this effort is that you work personally with volunteers from other departments in a project environment. Few, if any, of the people you meet in such organizations are likely to be in a position to advance your career immediately. But the awareness you create at this time for your name and personal qualities is likely to serve you well later on. (We are aware of numerous individuals who were asked for by parallel departmental groups—Promotion to Advertising, for example—as the result of this type of exposure.)

While the chances of working with people in more senior positions than your own on such civic-minded projects are not great, they do exist. One of our outplaced clients told us how his perseverance as a solicitor for his company's blood bank earned him a position in the sales department. It seems the chairman of the blood bank committee was none other than his company's national sales manager. Another client's efforts on a credit union committee led to a promotion into the treasury department.

Perhaps the greatest opportunity for demonstrating personal qualities to people in key positions in a company comes by joining company teams. The Chief Financial Officer of a $25,000,000 computer peripherals company, for example, loved bowling and so did a young trainee in the company's intern program for college seniors. The bond developed outside the office led to an invitation on graduation for this person to become the C.F.O.'s first full-time administrative assistant, which eventually led to a supervisory position for the young bowler years ahead of others who joined the company at the same time he did.

If you're not a sports person, you'll be glad to know teams are not the only way to contact senior people whom you wouldn't otherwise rub shoulders with. One female accounting supervisor, for example, worked on the employee newspaper published every month at her plant. In this capacity, she suggested to the editor that they do a feature story on each department head at the plant so that workers could get to know them better. The editor, a member of the personnel department, loved the idea and asked the accounting supervisor to interview these key people. The impression she made on her boss's boss's boss while writing her story about the Chief Financial Officer led to her being recommended for promotion a few weeks later—which she claimed she would otherwise not have been considered for!

The secret of creating awareness in any organization is to find ways to meet and know more people, even if this involves a little extra effort. You may not really *want* to attend the dull company picnic, you may have better things to do than represent your department at a meeting called to improve overcrowding in the parking lot, and so on. But if you look upon such things as elements of your personal advancement campaign, you'll probably find that in the long run they're worth it!

Developing Friendships with Members of Your Organization Who Share Common Backgrounds

It is common sense that if there are people at higher levels in your organization who went to the same school you did or previously worked at the same company as you did, or came from the same part of the country as you are from, you have a built-in reason to introduce yourself to these people and, as the need arises, to seek their advice and counsel. You may, perhaps, frown on the idea of introducing yourself to fellow alumni(ae) in your company who have advanced beyond the organizational level you are now at. You might feel, for example, that taking advantage of common past associations to gain access to potential bosses and mentors is not really a fair way to get yourself ahead. If you do feel this way, consider just two things. First, if people are fond of their alma mater to start with, they usually grow fonder with age. Thus, senior people may be genuinely delighted when a newcomer to a company takes the time and effort to bring them up to date on their alma mater or to update them on how things are back home. You are, in fact, doing such persons a kind act in going to see them!

Second, and just as important, as was pointed out in an earlier chapter, it is a fact of life that people are more likely to purchase an item they are familiar with. Thus, by letting potential mentors know of your similar backgrounds, you make their selection process easier. Not taking advantage of common past associations not only deprives you of an important personal advantage you have in selling yourself, but it also deprives the senior people of the advantages of such ties as well!

SUSTAINING AWARENESS

As suggested earlier, in packaged goods marketing creating awareness for a new brand or product is only the beginning; sustaining awareness is also critical to a brand's long-term success. (Reaching a potential customer once with your advertising message is usually not enough to create a sale.) You need to reinforce recall of your message so that your potential buyer will think immediately of your brand at the time he or she goes to the store to make a purchase.

As suggested at the beginning of this chapter, the need to sustain awareness of you is even more important in personal marketing than it is in packaged goods. That's because people usually go back into the marketplace for aspirin and toothpaste every few weeks or months, but mentors may not be looking to fill positions more than once every several years. Thus, you have to keep your name in their minds for long periods in order to take advantage of the awareness you created using one or more of the ten techniques described above. This isn't easy to do. You can't very well run reminder ads about you as you might do in selling a packaged goods brand. Nonetheless, there are several things you might try to keep your name favorably in potential sponsors' or bosses' minds. Here are some examples:

Sending Articles You Believe May Be of Professional Interest to Someone You Met

When you think about it, it only takes a moment or two to clip a piece from the paper or a trade journal. But it does take a special mindset; you have to be aware of the interests (professional and otherwise) of acquaintances and make it your business to cut the article out and forward it to them.

Is it worth it? As you make this decision, consider that this effort is living proof of the kind of person you really are. Clipping an article says to the recipient that you are genuinely interested in the people you meet and that you care enough about them to go out of your way to help them be more productive in their jobs. Thus, your effort will not only keep your name in their minds, but it is likely to reinforce a favorable image of you!

Making Acquaintances Aware of Job Opportunities You Learn of, Whenever You Think There's Even a Remote Chance Your Acquaintance Could Be Interested in the Position

It has been proven statistically that today word of mouth is the single largest source of candidates for available positions, and learning about these opportunities is the first critical step in the traditional job search process. By making appropriate acquaintances aware of job openings you learn of from executive recruiters, associates, and friends, you demonstrate a concern for these acquaintances that should make these people remember you kindly even if they are not interested in pursuing the position! We are aware of one manufacturing executive who regularly reads the want ads for acquaintances as well as for himself! Unusual? You bet. But when he sends clippings of exceptional jobs to former peers, he is building a residue of goodwill that has to stand him in good stead in the future.

Going Out of Your Way To Help Peers Who Contact You During a Job Serach

Because so few job opportunities are advertised, putting peers in touch with acquaintances of yours whom they do not know can aid them significantly to secure a new job. Actively assisting your friends in networking (as this sourcing system is commonly called) can benefit you in two ways. Not only will it help you be remembered by the peer who seeks the names of people who might know of jobs, but it will also be remembered by those people whom you recommend that your peers contact! (When Bill Jones calls an acquaintance of Jim Smith's and says "Jim Smith suggested I call," Jim Smith is getting a personal plug with this acquaintance, even though Bill Jones is the one doing the job search!) So, if you're asked for names by a peer who is networking, going out of your way to think of three or four people this peer should contact will actually help you stay in touch with your own acquaintances who could be important to your success down the road.

Keeping Executive Recruiters Advised of What You Are Currently Doing

Today, a good many executive recruiting firms maintain data banks on qualified career people. By having information on file about the experience and skills of particular candidates, these firms are able to fill positions for their clients sooner and at less cost. If you've changed companies in the past and sent out resumes, your name is likely to be in such a file. If you have ever received a phone call or letter from a recruiting firm inquiring about your interest in a particular job in your field, you know your name is on file, too.

Unfortunately, most career people don't bother to keep recruiters up to date on what they are doing. This can be a costly mistake. Unless executive recruiters seeking persons with your background know where to find you, you obviously won't be considered for opportunities that might well interest you. And if you don't make executive recruiters aware of new job titles and new company experience garnered since your last job search, they are unlikely to contact you concerning openings requiring this more recent experience even if they know how to get in touch!

Thus, it makes good sense to write a note every year to every recruiter and professional employment counsellor whom you have befriended during the past. Let him or her know you aren't on the job market, but that you just wanted to let him or her know what you're up to. This could take only a few minutes to do if you set it up on a word processor or a few hours of your time, if you don't, but it may be the best investment in maintaining awareness of you outside your present company that you could ever make!

By Attending Meetings Regularly of Those Professional Organizations You Belong To

The more times you chat with members of your profession, the greater the likelihood they will know who you are in the event that someone in your field is looking for you. Enough said!

By Sending Christmas Cards

The 20¢ stamp and the 50¢ Christmas card put a real dent in Christmas card sending. And that can work to your advantage. If once a year you write a personal note on your card to people you don't see regularly, your chances of maintaining awareness is obviously better. It may seem corny to write to an old acquaintance saying "I didn't want the year to end without just saying hi," but it's the sort of message that makes people feel good, particularly during the holiday season.

By Systematically Calling
Every Acquaintance You've Met

You may have trouble seeing yourself making a phone call each day to someone you worked with in the past or met at a professional or social organization and with whom you would like to stay in touch, but we have met a number of executives who have elaborate systems for doing just this. And, incidentally, they seem to enjoy these contacts immensely. It may be that it takes something of a politician's mentality to do this. But if you do, you'll never need to conduct a traditional job search; of that you can be certain.

There are, of course, many other things you might do to stay in touch. We know of a secretary turned executive who made it her business to send birthday cards to almost everyone she ever worked for or with— hundreds each month; a salesman who wrote a "Personal Note" on the anniversary of each sale he made; a stockbroker who literally scoured *The Wall Street Journal, New York Times, Forbes,* and *Dun's Review* each and every day, clipping every item in which a college classmate or former business associate's name appeared and then wrote a letter of congratulations to each person. (It was his sole hobby.)

The point is not how you stay in touch with people you have met, but that you do make it your business to maintain awareness of your name in a positive way with as many peers and potential mentors as you possibly can. You never know when one of these people will think of you for a career-advancing opportunity in his or her own organization or will recommend you for a similar opportunity with a friend in another organization.

If you have ever conducted a traditional job search, you know how important former friendships can be. You may well have secured your present position through networking to these friends—more than one in four jobs is secured this way. Now, think for a moment how much more effective your traditional job search might have been had you made it your business to develop more contacts when you weren't conducting a job search and to keep in touch with these people more frequently than you have in the past so that your friendships were deeper. Your traditional job search would surely have been shorter.

If for no reason other than this, a campaign to create and maintain awareness when you aren't looking for a job makes good sense. And here's the best plus of all: if you do a good enough job of creating awareness of your name with sufficient numbers of people and demonstrate your personal interest in them by staying in touch in a meaningful way, you probably won't ever need to conduct a traditional job search again! Awareness of you and personal interest in you (a halo effect of your interest in your associates) is likely to make this unnecessary.

STAYING IN TOUCH WITH YOURSELF

1. Do you have a systematic plan for building awareness of your name outside your own organization?

2. How many of the seven intercompany awareness techniques described in this chapter can you honestly say you employ on a regular basis to create awareness of you?

3. Do you have a systematic plan for building awareness of your name inside your present organization?

4. How many of the three intracompany awareness techniques described in this chapter can you honestly say you employ on a regular basis?

5. Do you have a systematic plan for maintaining awareness of your name in a positive way?

6. How many of the seven recall-reinforcement techniques do you employ on a regular basis?

7. Considering both the ten awareness-creating techniques and the seven recall-reinforcement devices described in this chapter, what would be the simplest, most suitable way for you to develop and sustain new, potentially career-advancing acquaintanceships at this time?

8. Will you commit yourself to such a program? Why do you say this?

chapter ten

Maximizing your long-term potential in the success market

If you've answered the questions at the end of each chapter, you should be feeling a new sense of power over your future. And with good reason, since you have developed a better understanding of:

1. The rational and irrational things that motivate bosses and mentors as they select people like you for promotions and development.

2. Your ability to deliver meaningful corporate and personal benefits to those people who control your future in your present organization.

3. The critical nature of the image you project to those people who can have an impact on your success.

4. What you can do now to improve your ability to deliver more meaningful benefits, and just as important, to enhance the image you create as a supplier of benefits both inside and outside your present organization.

5. The potential markets for your experience, training, and talents that you could realistically pursue if your analysis of your saleability in your own organization leads you to consider other options.

6. How you can significantly increase the number of potential buyers who are aware of the benefits, perceived and actual, that you might deliver to them.

If you consider these six items carefully in making your plans, you can't help but compete more successfully. And, hence, your feeling of confidence about the future. How far you make it up the ladder of success, however, may depend on three additional variables which have an impact on every marketing program. These variables are positioning, timing, and pricing.

POSITIONING TO ADVANCE YOUR CAREER

Positioning is a packaged goods marketing technique that involves concentrating a brand's total selling efforts against a portion or segment of total buyers in a product category in order to increase the brand's total sales and share within the entire product category. Virginia Slims is an example of positioning at work. In case you are not familiar with this brand, it is an extra-long cigarette. As such, its makers could have tried to compete against all other long cigarettes for a share of total sales. But they didn't. Instead, they opted to have Virginia Slims compete in less than half the total cigarette market! The piece of the pie that Virginia Slims concentrated its efforts on included assertive, career-oriented, female smokers. To this end, the makers of Virginia Slims designed a slim, oval cigarette in a sophisticated pastel package that research told them would appeal directly to this target audience. Of course, in doing so, this significantly reduced the brand's appeal to male smokers and traditional female smokers. What's more, Virginia Slims advertising appealed directly to women who either considered themselves liberated or wished to become liberated—a fraction of all female smokers in any case.

Were the makers of Virginia Slims crazy to restrict their marketing focus so drastically? Yes, like a fox! By positioning their brand against this limited audience, they were infinitely more effective in creating loyal Virginia Slims buyers in this small segment of the total cigarette market than they would have been had they introduced another also-ran cigarette which appealed to no one in particular in the total smoking market. In summary, they were successful because they aimed at becoming a big frog in a small, selective pond rather than attempting to be just another frog in a large pond.

Virginia Slims is by no means the only brand to build sales by limiting its marketing focus. Palmolive Liquid is a dishwashing detergent. To look at their advertising, however, you'd think it was a cuticle softener. Its makers limited its appeal to those people concerned more about the look of their hands than the look of their dishes. In contrast, Janitor-in-a-Drum is positioned as an industrial-strength cleanser. As such, it appeals to homemakers interested in getting cleansing chores done fast and with the least amount of elbow grease. In contrast to Palmolive Liquid, its makers sacrificed sales to buyers worried about the impact of a strong, industrial cleanser on their skin. The fascinating thing is that both of these products sold more by limiting their focus to that portion of the market in which the manufacturer believed it could most effectively compete.

In personal marketing, positioning can be just as important to your long-term success. To utilize this technique, you have to adopt an attitude that says you'll no longer compete in the total job market and no longer respond to every ad that calls for a person with one aspect of your background and/or skills. Instead, you'll concentrate your efforts exclusively on those few, selected job universes that you believe could genuinely benefit from the unique combination of your experience, training, talents, and interests. At a minimum, you'll seek out and pursue only those companies, job titles, and/or industries that require at least two elements of your total package. Shown below are possible pairings you might consider in evaluating how you could position your past in order to compete more effectively in the future, along with real-life examples that demonstrate how this pairing has worked to provide career people like yourself with a competitive edge in the limited job universes they elected to pursue.

A Combination of Two Different Skills

Bryan O. was a commercial artist with limited success in two advertising areas. He spent the first eight years of his career as an illustrator for a commercial art firm. The job demanded great skill in rendering people in different industrial settings. Recognizing that his talent for drawing exciting illustrations was not good enough to move him ahead in this field, Bryan switched careers by securing a job as an art director in a large ad agency where he did rough layouts and T.V. commercial storyboards. The job didn't require an illustrator's flair so Bryan thought he'd do well at it. He discovered that he had quite a talent for turning out good layouts. But, unfortunately, Bryan did not have the facility for batting them out quickly—a requirement in the advertising agency business with its tight timetables.

After several years of average performance reviews as a layout person, Bryan asked himself what types of firms might need a person with adequate ability at both layouts and illustrations. Bryan decided to pursue smaller manufacturing companies that did their own advertising or promotion, figuring that such companies would require both skills but Bryan eventually became the art department for a $25,000,000 direct mail catalog operation—a position in which he excelled and which brought him not only financial rewards, but a feeling of great accomplishment as well.

A Combination of Two Different Kinds of Experience

Ken I. worked 20 years in a major New York bank. His progress was limited because he did not have a bachelor's degree. In this prestigious banking firm, his high-school image was such that he was never considered for an officership in the pension administration department in which he worked. Nonetheless, Lawrence was bright and hardworking and knew the ins and outs of investment banking better than many of his peers.

About ten years into his banking career, Lawrence was frustrated enough to ask for and pursue a position as an administrator in the bank's newly expanded computer department. Again, Lawrence excelled in lower-level positions but was never given a managerial role because the bank still looked upon him as a capable enlisted man and nothing more.

Now 20 years into his career and in his 40's, Lawrence decided to leave his bank and try his luck elsewhere. His first thought was to ply his skills at other banks that he hoped might accept him for his experience rather than his image. Then he decided on a different option. He knew the investment banking business inside out. And he knew computer operations within the banking industry like the palm of his hand. Lawrence decided to pursue companies selling computers and computer programs to the investment banking industry, figuring that his experience in both areas might make him valuable. And, he reasoned, computer companies might not be so concerned about his noncollege background.

Lawrence's job campaign paid off. He joined a large data processing company as marketing manager for the banking industry. In this capacity, he was responsible for developing new computer services for banks like the one he had worked at for 20 years. In his new company, hard work and good ideas were sufficient to get Lawrence promoted to director of market development for all computer services created by his company, and he nearly doubled his salary within four years of leaving the bank. His experience in banking and computers had been sold to the right buyer!

A Combination of Experience and Training

Naomi L. had a masters degree in psychology before she decided to get married and raise a family, thereby ending her academic career to stay at home. As a result, she never pursued her doctorate degree. A decade later, following a divorce, she entered the workforce seeking a position that would utilize her psychological training. Without her doctorate, the best she could find was a job as a group counsellor in a mental health clinic operated by a social services agency. The job of helping minority women to better adjust to life was interesting for Naomi, but it paid next to nothing.

During the course of her work, Naomi came up with a new concept in group therapy. She brought her clients together to watch T.V. soap operas and used this device to help them better understand and cope with the emotional stresses that they faced. Within a year or two, Naomi had gained some national recognition for her soap opera approach to counselling and had several articles written about her.

It was at this point that Naomi decided the time had come to pursue other career options that might pay a decent wage. She reviewed her situation and elected to pursue only film-producing firms that might want someone with her unique combination of psychological training and experience analyzing the emotional content of dramas. Naomi believed she would be very valuable to a film producer trying to select scripts that would enjoy high viewer involvement and, hence, sales. Naomi secured such a position with a movie studio which produced T.V. soap operas.

The interesting things about this are that Naomi more than doubled her salary by making this career change, and she created her position by communicating the benefits of what she did to a company that previously did not have a psychologist on its staff. Incidentally, Naomi's current firm has seen an increase in sales thanks to Naomi who now uses her group technique to evaluate plots for pilot programs to determine their potential before hundreds of thousands of dollars are invested in actors, sets, and celluloid. Naomi couldn't be happier. And neither could her employer who is taking advantage of both her theoretical training and practical experience to make his operation more profitable!

A Combination of Business Experience and Avocational Interests

Jim P. worked for about eight years with one of the largest retail chains in the U.S. He was smart, good with people, and hardworking. This combination brought him from a sales position to that of manager of a very large auto repair and service facility owned and operated by this retail chain. As a manager, he was also very successful. His merchandising flair enabled him to build tire, battery, and service sales in the service center from about $4,000,000 to $8,000,000 in about three years!

It was at this point in his career that Jim decided that he wanted out of the retailing business, that he no longer wanted to manage an auto-service facility, and that he wanted to get involved in product marketing. As he thought of alternative buyers who might want him, he also considered his extraordinary knowledge of the music industry that resulted from his 15 years of systematically collecting records and tapes of rock and country music. Jim asked himself how he could parlay both his knowledge of the auto-service business and interest in musical trends. He decided to pursue marketing opportunities in recording companies that might be interested in building tape sales through new kinds of retail outlets.

Jim eventually secured a position with one of the newer firms in the industry. In his position, Jim was responsible for merchandising popular cassettes within auto-service centers! Jim reports directly to the director of marketing, and at last report, was very happy about the career shift since it capitalized on both prior vocational experience and his lifelong pastime.

STEPS TO MAKE POSITIONING
WORK IN PERSONAL MARKETING

As you read over these four case histories, several conclusions may strike you about positioning as a technique for advancing your career. First, the technique is nothing more than practical application of the benefits corrollary outlined in Chapter 1 that stated that if you can offer users more than one benefit, you are likely to do better in the marketplace than your competition that offers only one. The second conclusion you might reach is that to make positioning work to enhance your own career requires a good deal of thought, effort, and good luck. This is probably the case, too. But this technique is likely to help any career person like yourself if you approach the task systematically and complete each of these straightforward steps.

Identification of Possible Pairings of Skills, Experience, Image, and Interest That Might Provide You with a Competitive Edge

This isn't complex. All you have to do is objectively analyze each of the individual successes you have had in the past, both at work and in other endeavors, and try to determine what factors about you made for success in these particular instances. If you see any consistent elements coming into play in a project or assignment in which the boss said you stood out, you'll have a pretty good idea of what special characteristics about you might work for you day in and day out in the right job universe.

Identification of Particular Job Universes in Which Your Special Combination of Talents, Experience, Image, and Interests Might Provide You with the Greatest Competitive Edge

This could take some creativity on your part. It also might take describing your particular benefit combinations to close friends and acquaintances and seeking their suggestions.

Exploring the Probabilities of Your Success
in the Alternative Job Universes You
Come Up With as Possible Markets
for Your Unique Set of Skills, Experience,
and So On

Read job descriptions in the *Dictionary of Occupational Titles,* a reference text in almost any good business library. As you read over these job descriptions, ask yourself whether what you would bring to each job would be significantly more than the next person. Another way of determining your competitive position—and probably a better one—would be to seek introductions to people already successful in the positions or industries you think you might like to pursue. Get their input as to what factors make for success in their fields and functions; they're in a position to know. Finding people in the industries or positions you might pursue may take some leg-work on your part, but if you ask your immediate friends for referrals, it can be done.

Pinpointing Specific Job Opportunities
Within the Field or Function
You Elect to Pursue

It is possible that the successful people you sought out in your research may know about openings in their fields. Chances are, however, that you'll need to build yourself a list of target companies. In doing so, the *Dun & Bradstreet Million Dollar Directory* can be very helpful. It's also available in most good business libraries, and as suggested in Chapter 3, all you need to do is find one company in the field you elect to pursue (perhaps the one the successful person you talked to works in) and you'll be able to find many similar companies. Were the D&B complete, it would be the only directory to use!

Experience has shown, however, that there are many companies that don't get listed in D&B because of their size or because they are components of larger organizations or conglomerates. Because of this, you might want to do some research in *The Directory of Directories.* It is one of the most remarkably useful sourcing tools ever developed. The current edition describes some 30,000 different directories you can purchase that list specific industries and specific functional groups and provides data on the cost of such directories and how you can obtain them.

You might also do some research in the *Encyclopedia of Associations*. You would be astounded at the number of professional and industry groups existing in the U.S. The encyclopedia provides you with sufficient information to get in touch with groups of interest to you. Often, such groups have association membership rosters which are an instant source of people and companies you could contact in the particular field you pursue.

Conducting a Job Campaign Against Your Target Job Market

This won't be easy, particularly if you are pursing a totally different field than the one you are now in, one you think will be more likely to recognize the advantages you bring to it. In pursuing your campaign, *How to Get a Better Job Quicker* (Taplinger) probably will be of help. Even with this guide, it will take a lot of work. It will take dogged pursuit of companies that don't yet recognize that they could make use of you, as was Naomi's experience. It may take good salesmanship to convince the right person to take a chance on you as was Jim's experience. It may take a critical self-evaluation of your limitations as was the case with Bryan. And finally, it could take some plain dumb luck, as was probably the case with Larry who happened to run into a data processing firm that was trying to get a foothold in the banking industry.

Is positioning a worthwhile personal marketing tool in your own case? If you have already gained experience in two different industries and doubt that your ability to provide benefits (real or imagined) is likely to give you a competitive edge in either, it is certainly worth exploring how you can put the two kinds of experience together to explore opportunities in yet a third job universe. On the other hand, if you have had experience in only one field and have decided objectively that your benefits capability or image in this field limit your chances for long-term success, then it would pay for you to consider alternative job universes in any event.

As you select alternative fields to pursue, keep in mind that you might not succeed in this second career either. As such, one factor to consider in making your choice of a new job is how well it complements the experience and skills you acquired from your previous job. Keep in mind that it could be the skills in the first two job universes combined together and used in still a third success marketplace that could give you your competitive advantage.

If you have no intention of leaving your present company, it would still pay for you to keep positioning in mind as you select between promotional opportunities. Each time you consider alternative job offers within your company, ask yourself not only which one provides the most immediate benefits (title, money, job satisfaction), but also which one would provide you with the greatest long-term leverage when combined with your experience to date. If you are able to secure a position internally that brings with it a different and complementary set of skills or knowledge than those you have gained in your present position, in five or ten years from now you may be in a position to combine these two sets of experience to provide significantly greater benefits to your company or to create a significantly superior image than your competition. If you question the value of this approach, check the backgrounds of some of the people at the top of your outfit. See if they represent a combination of positions (engineering plus manufacturing; domestic plus international; finance plus treasury; and so on). In many companies it is just this strategy that has enabled the people who made it to the top to position themselves to provide greater benefits to their employer, and hence, create for themselves a competitive edge in advancing their careers.

TIMING AS A FACTOR IN PERSONAL MARKETING

The second marketing variable this chapter explores is timing. You probably don't need to be convinced of the importance of timing in packaged goods market success. Being first to provide a new benefit can be crucial in winning buyer loyalty. As a case in point, chances are you've never heard of Cue toothpaste except for a casual reference in the introduction to this book. Yet it provided all the cavity-preventing benefits of Crest, and millions of dollars were spent to introduce it. Unfortunately, Cue was introduced a few months *after* Crest. Consequently, its promise was old hat, and within a year, Lever Brothers had withdrawn Cue from the marketplace.

On the other hand, being first isn't always the answer. Many a packaged goods brand has failed to become an instant success because it was introduced too far in advance of consumer interest in the benefits it offered. Carlton cigarettes is such an example. It offered consumers the promise of less tar and nicotine for almost a decade before cigarette smokers became genuinely conscious of the health hazards of smoking, and during this period Carlton languished on the sidelines. Only in recent years has Carlton come into its own. And the Carlton experience is not singular. Today's health-conscious buyer seeks out high-fiber cereals at the supermarket. But a number of such cereals were available to buyers for years. These went nowhere—gathering dust on the shelves of the few health food stores that existed a decade ago—because they were introduced before many Americans became genuinely health conscious.

Timing can be just as crucial a factor in personal marketing. Two quick examples will convince you of this. The first concerns Tom Garth, a plant manager in a medical equipment manufacturing company. Tom was on a fast track with his company when he made up his mind to leave. Tom felt his career was stymied because his immediate boss, a group manufacturing director, had five years to go until retirement and hadn't been promoted in nearly ten years. Tom handed in his formal resignation when another company offered him the position of plant manager in a similar-sized plant to the one he had managed. Tom reasoned that in this new company he could probably secure a promotion in two years to the group level. As it turned out, *one week to the day* after Tom left, the boss who stymied his career was promoted into a staff position, and one of Tom's peers, a plant manager on less of a fast track than Tom, was promoted to group manufacturing director! Tom is kicking himself today, ten years later, for having left one week too soon.

The second example concerns Stan Birnbaum, a brilliant computer engineer who had been promoted from project manager, a line position in which a dozen computer applications engineers reported to him, to Manager of Engineering Finance. This latter position was at a higher level in Stan's organization but was a position in which he managed only four engineers and which was a staff function bridging the engineering and cost-accounting departments. After three years in this staff position, Stan was extremely frustrated. His position wasn't in the mainstream of his company's business; it required less engineering talent. Despite this, Stan stuck it out even so, primarily because a career counsellor told him that his saleability to other companies was very weak, and he had already put in for a transfer back to project management. In Stan's case, good timing paid off. Six months after he considered conducting a job search, he was promoted to group project manager, a two-grade promotion, which had 26 project managers reporting to him! Stan later found out that the staff position was a developmental position to groom him for his most recent promotion.

When it comes to timing the advances in your own career, there are no perfect answers. This book does, however, have five timing suggestions that could work to your advantage.

Make Personal Marketing a Continuing Effort

As stated, the traditional approach of entering the job market every three or four years is just plain inefficient. You should be doing something consciously at all times to move yourself ahead. Whether it's auditing your image, benefits capability, and credentials against competition; undertaking a personal development program to prepare yourself to compete better; exploration of opportunity markets in which you could more effectively compete; or developing awareness of you by potential buyers inside and outside your present company, do something every day, every week, every month, to keep up with or get ahead of competition in the success market in which you compete.

Be Patient in Your Desire for Results

In business, there's an old rule of thumb, often quoted by consultants, that says career people should take a step forward one year for every ten years they've lived. Applying that formula to your own career means that if you are in your 20's wait at least two years in your present position for your boss or mentor to promote you into a position in which you can develop new skills; three years in your 30's; four years in your 40's, and five years in your 50's. If you are one of those people who is frustrated after one year because you haven't advanced your career, keep this rule of thumb in mind.

Personal marketing is slow marketing for three reasons: First, the development of the product (you) is gradual. Second, buying opportunities for people like you don't happen daily. They tend to bunch up around the time when someone in the organization leaves, creating a sort of musical chairs series of organizational shifts. And, finally, developing awareness of you by potential buyers is, as discussed in the previous chapter, a long, drawn-out process.

Add these three factors together, and you can readily understand why upward movement within an organization takes time. Not only do you have to grow to deserve promotion, but you have to wait until a situation in which your corporate or personal benefits can be rewarded by someone whom you've befriended along the way. Among the people who our firm has outplaced are a great many who wished they hadn't left a previous organization as quickly as they did—people who knew objectively that they wanted too much too soon, but who on a nonrational basis raced to find new corporate homes, only to discover that long-term opportunities were not greener in the other pasture, as they had hoped they might be.

Be Conscious of the Need to Develop; Don't Bide Your Time Too Long

In the very same breath as this book admonishes you to have patience, it urges you not to wait too long at any one point in your career for your mentors or your boss to help move you ahead! A contradiction? Not really.

In packaged goods marketing, the P&Gs of this world are very much concerned with their products becoming old hat. They know that "new" and "improved" are key words to persuade potential buyers to try their products, long after their introduction. Thus, they update packages or create "new, 20% stronger" labels every couple of years.

There's a strong parallel in personal marketing. If you've remained too long in the same position, you run the risk of developing an image within your organization as someone who is no longer capable of further growth—someone who has plateaued in his or her career. To put it another way, unless you are moving upwards, you may not be perceived as being capable of continuing to do so! Thus, the suggestion is made that you keep an eye out for clues to your progress by asking yourself questions like these:

- Are any of your peers moving more rapidly than you are?
- Have you been passed over for a promotion you thought you would get?
- Are your annual reviews less good now than in the past (even though they may be more than satisfactory)?
- Was your promotion to your present position really a lateral move into a job that provides no more opportunities for advancement than the one you were previously in?

If your answer to any of these questions is "yes," you should put your career-advancing efforts into high gear. If you have determined that your image is such within your present company that it could not be improved in spite of a personal development campaign to enable you to offer more corporate or personal benefits or a better shelf package, then a traditional job search campaign may be called for. If you honestly believe that you can upgrade your image and ability to provide more corporate and/or personal benefits within your organization, don't delay for one minute working on a crash self-development program. And start to locate new potential buyers within your organization who need to know your name before it's too late to find any buyers at all.

When You Enlist the Aid of Mentors and Bosses to Help You Advance Your Career, Give Them Time to Make Things Happen

Tom Garth, the plant manager who left too soon, did approach a key manufacturing executive in his firm a month before he submitted his resignation. Tom was well regarded by this individual, and Tom was told something would be done for him. But a month was not long enough for the organizational changes involving Tom to be finalized. Even if your boss is solidly behind you, it can take six months or a year to create the opportunity you are looking for. The market for people is not like the market for bread or cigarettes in which buying opportunities develop daily. The market for people is much more like the market for a hay fever remedy or a stye medicine. It develops infrequently only when the need arises. So when you set a date for yourself to move up a notch in your success market, keep the date flexible.

Impatience with mentors and bosses has caused many a career person to leave an environment in which they have developed a positive image for themselves only to join new organizations in which they have no image at all, and no potential buyers except for those people who brought them aboard. In cases like these, the career-advancement time saved in switching companies is often lost many times over in establishing a buying market within the new organization in which these people compete. Before you jump ship, ask yourself if the time advantage you anticipate in developing your career is real and not imagined.

Be Conscious of Potential Opportunities Early Enough to Do Something About Them

If you think or have reason to believe your boss may be leaving in a few months, assess your chances of being promoted to the vacancy. If you doubt that it is coming your way, as things stand, ask yourself if you can do anything to improve the odds prior to the decision on who will replace your boss. Quite possibly, you can change your image in a few months if you take dramatic steps to do so. Perhaps, in the intervening period you can develop greater awareness of you by someone who you may feel will be involved in the decision on whom to promote. Maybe you can improve your chances by providing more personal benefits to the person or people involved in the decision.

Be conscious, too, of shifts within the organization that could lead to the development of new opportunities for you. A new product line, for example, could mean expansion of manufacturing facilities and an opportunity for a shift superintendent to advance to plant manager, and so on. The secret of seizing this type of opportunity lies in analyzing your chances to secure the potential promotion, if it materializes. That may take nothing more than intensifying your awareness campaign to decision makers, or it could take nothing less than enrolling in a specialized course to prepare yourself to be considered for the potential opportunity.

Obviously, your first step is to become totally aware of potential shifts in your organization's strategy that could lead to opportunities. Then, and only then, can you take appropriate action in time to benefit from your advance knowledge of the situation. Incidentally, in keeping yourself in tune with potential developments within your company that could create opportunities for you, you are doing something very akin to what successful packaged goods marketers do—anticipating buying desires so that products can be formulated to meet these emerging needs. It works for packaged goods manufacturers; it makes sense to make it work for you!

PRICING AS A FACTOR
IN PERSONAL MARKETING

When you read earlier that pricing was the third variable influencing long-term success to be discussed in this chapter, you may have been somewhat surprised. After all, the seventh packaged goods success principle reviewed way back in Chapter 1 clearly states that winning brands almost invariably achieved their success based on selling value—*not* on price. What's more, Chapter 2 was clear in stating that this same value principle applied to successful people, too. Given this background, you might well wonder why pricing (or compensation, as price tags for people is called) is even discussed at all.

The fact is that compensation is almost *never* a factor in the success of those people who make it to the top in their fields by growing in just one company. After all, when your bosses or mentors make choices as to who to promote or develop, they don't concern themselves with which subordinate has the lowest income, and hence, is the best bargain in terms of development. Rather, your bosses select people to bring along based on perceived value to the organization in the long run. This, of course, is based on the benefits, corporate and personal, that you or other subordinates actually delivered in the past and the belief created by you or other subordinates that you or they have the potential for delivering benefits in the future. (This belief is usually related to image.) Compensation is less of an issue, too, when career people remain within a single industry.

Whether you get asked to join another company based on a traditional job search or through an ongoing awareness campaign, in most cases your prospective boss knows that he or she will have to meet what competition pays in order to lure you away.

So, you ask, where does pricing become a factor in personal marketing? And how does it relate to value? Fortunately, the packaged goods business provides the answers. Consider, if you will, toothpaste. Within this product group, the most successful brands do compete on value as we've seen previously. (Crest offered the first fluoride protection long ago to secure its number one position; Aqua-fresh came along more recently and offered mouthwash protection and fluoride protection, and cut drastically into Crest's business). Neither brand competes based on price. In fact, both command premium price tags and still hold larger market shares than the "store's own" brands that sell for a good deal less!

So, where *does* price competition become a factor? Not between toothpaste brands but between the different types of stores that sell toothpaste. If you went to one of those discount department stores like Zayre's or Bradlee's, for example, you would be likely to find all toothpastes priced less than at food or drug stores that traditionally have priced these packaged goods at manufacturer's suggested retail. On the other hand, if you were to shop for toothpaste at convenience stores like 7-Eleven, AM/PM, or Quik-Mart, you would likely pay somewhat more than the suggested retail prices for all of the toothpaste brands. And if per chance you run out of toothpaste at a hotel and try to buy some in the shop in the lobby, you could well end up paying almost twice what you would in a food or drug outlet. (The merchant here knows that he or she has a captive market for all brands.)

In sum, then, compensation becomes a far more important factor in marketing yourself depending on where you market yourself (e.g., if you elect to leave your own industry than if you grow yourself in it). And this is true whether you decide to leave because you conclude that your ability to provide benefits (real or perceived) is greater outside your own industry or because you want more money than your industry is willing to pay you. In this case, as in packaged goods marketing, where you sell yourself (the type of industry you try to join) will have an impact on your compensation. If you do choose to market your talents in an industry other than the one you are now in, keep these pricing variables in mind.

Different Industries Have Traditionally Paid a Higher Price for Talented People Than Other Industries Seeking the Same Talented People

Sounds crazy, but it's true, and our firm has worked with hundreds of out-placed persons whose training and skills would bring them far more dollars in one field than another. One example makes a telling point: Dan Boyer was a portfolio manager with a leading asset management firm. His salary in that organization was $65,000. Dan's experience was equally appropriate as a portfolio manager for a bank trust department. The maximum offer he received from a bank to manage a portfolio much the same size as the one he had already managed in the firm he was leaving was $45,000. Dan's experience and talent were equally appropriate to yet a third field—in a corporation that managed its own pension fund. In this marketplace, Dan received an offer of $55,000 to manage a portfolio of comparable size to the one he had managed. In still a fourth marketplace—the brokerage firms—Dan received offers in the $85,000 range!

Why compensation differentials exist between different industries is not all that clear, but they do. And the starting salaries for M.B.A.'s is another testament to this fact. Year after year the retailing and banking industries have been lower bidders for quality talent than manufacturing companies. And year after year the financial organizations on and off Wall Street and consulting firms have offered even more still. Is it any wonder so few Harvard M.B.A.'s enter the retailing or banking businesses! Differentials in other industries are more easily explained: the airlines and travel firms, for example, can afford to pay less because peripheral benefits are generally greater. And the glamour industries like television, advertising, and newspapers can afford to start writers at less than the plain-jane manufacturing companies pay writers with similar creative skills to produce and edit internal communications (magazines, stockholder reports, newsletters, and so on.) On the other hand, experienced advertising copywriters can generally count on higher salaries than people with comparable wordcrafting skills who work for trade magazines, and so on.

Obviously these kinds of differentials could have an impact on your long-term market value, if you consider alternate job universes to the one you are now in. So if you elect to explore other job arenas, make yourself aware of the price tags generally put on people with your kind of talent, training, and level of experience. How can you find this out? If you have any friends in employment agencies or recruiting firms, they may be able to give you the answer directly. Or, alternately, you could contact the U.S. Department of Labor District Office nearest you. Periodically, this department publishes salary ranges for jobs within different industries, and you can compare comparable positions in each. As a final suggestion, check your bookstore or library for reference books on this topic. There are a number of guides for young people that also provide industry-by-industry salary ranges. A little time spent in checking price tags on your talent now might make a difference of thousands of dollars of income over your lifetime.

Large Companies Have Traditionally Paid a Higher Price Tag Than Small Companies for People in the Very Same Positions

Numerous firms conduct compensation surveys sold to company personnel departments that are trying to find out if they are paying competitive wages within their industry. Some of these studies compare pay for the same jobs in different-sized companies. And while you might expect big companies to be able to offer more to their employees, you'd be amazed at the enormity of the differences! As a rule of thumb, companies with sales under $5,000,000 pay half as much (or less) as companies in the $500,000,000 plus bracket pay for people in similar titles!

If you are considering leaving your company and are interested in what different-sized organizations in your field are paying, check your library for *Dartnell's Annual Executive Compensation Survey*. If you can't find it, you can buy it directly from Dartnell's Chicago headquarters for under $100. You might also ask your librarian about Siddons Company compensation studies. Usually these are sold directly to companies, and you may not find copies readily available. Siddon's overall summary could be in some business libraries, however, and you might also try contacting a friend who works in a company compensation department. It could make valuable reading. Some professional associations—I.E.E.E. and A.S.P.A., to name just two—also conduct studies of what their members earn in different industries and different-sized companies. It would pay to find out if the professional society in your career field has made such a study and get your hands on a copy!

Industry Conditions Can Impact On Salaries, Too

While many firms wish to keep competitive with other firms in and out of their fields, financial pressures can lead to periodic situations in which their salary ranges are well out of whack. In the automotive industry, for example, which has traditionally tried to bid competitively for high-tech engineers in good times; wage freezes across the board to all professional employees have made it virtually impossible for these companies to offer competitive salaries to new employees who were sought to fill such positions. These companies' compensation departments have been caught on the horns of a dilemma. They know better than to offer new hires more than they now pay employees on the payroll who have comparable jobs. And because of across-the-board wage freezes or cuts, these companies are not paying employees as much as their counterparts in competitive industries.

If you are thinking of switching industries, check the long-term trends in profitability for leading firms in the fields you're considering. You may well decide that while one industry might pay you more now for your experience and skills, in the long run it wouldn't be able to keep up the differential.

Salary Scales Can Have Significant Geographic Differences

If you are considering leaving the company you're in now to increase your income, where you conduct your search can have a big difference on your long-term earnings potential. This is true because so many companies consider the local cost of living in their compensation formulas as well as what competitors in their industry are paying. Our files contain case after case in which people left their companies because they were offered 15% to 25% more by other firms, only to find out later that because the jobs they took were in California, Boston, New York, or other high-cost-of-living cities, their standards of living didn't increase one iota! It works the other way around, too. Our files also turn up instances in which career people have settled for little or no salary increases when they switched jobs but who still came out far ahead in their purchasing power because they concentrated their searches in areas of the country where the cost-of-living was substantially less than where they had been working.

It would pay for every career person considering changing jobs to analyze all four variables whether he or she switches companies or industries.

Pricing Dilemmas

There is one other pricing question to ponder, too, in going after another position: What if you decide that you have a better chance for long-term success in an industry that pays significantly less than the one you are now in? Or your image is such that you might fare better in a smaller, more relaxed company that pays significantly smaller salaries, too? What should you do then?

Dan Boyers was in this kind of situation. He might easily have decided that banking was for him rather than asset management. If he had held out for his present salary of $65,000, he would probably have priced himself out of the banking business where $45,000 was the going price for his kind of experience and skills. What should you do in a dilemma like this? Your first thought might be to sell value and thus, trade up your prospective boss to a salary level consistent with what you made in your present job. But is it a realistic proposition? Probably not. After all, it's like asking the person who is considering a Chevrolet or a Ford to trade up to a Mercedes. He or she may be well aware of the superior quality of a Mercedes but just can't imagine coming up with that kind of money.

In marketing your talents, the problem of being overpriced is compounded by two facts. First, most companies have formal salary ranges for each position relative to other positions in the company. Thus, it would be very difficult to make an exception and pay you, say, $65,000 for what was pegged at a $45,000 job, because you might then earn more than the president! Obviously that wouldn't do! Second, many companies employ numbers of people in the same position. Again, it would be impossible to pay you $65,000 when everyone else in the same position was earning $45,000. Doing so would create a lot of unhappy people!

The tough question of being overpriced has confronted many outplaced persons we have worked with. Many ended up pursuing positions in industries in which they were less likely to succeed in the long run (based on deliverable benefits or image) just because these industries paid more! They did this not so much because they would have been strapped financially at a lower income, but because they were unable to deal with the problem of being perceived as worth less by another industry. (The lower salaries offered were seen as a personal affront to them.) Actually, the lower salaries they were offered had nothing whatsoever to do with them as individuals. It was simply a case of certain marketplaces not being willing to pay that much for a particular job category.

Do people who price themselves in one industry based on what they earned in another make a mistake in their quest for success? Our experience would suggest that they usually do! If a person has not been as successful in an industry as he or she thinks he or she should have been (which is often the case with those people our firm outplaces), continuing to go after jobs in this same industry because other industries may pay less for the same position is probably not in their best long-term interest. And that's simply because they are no more successful in their jobs the next time around!

The secret to long-term success is to match your benefits and image with the job market. If this means taking a lower price for your experience and talents in initially making a switch, it probably pays to do this. Getting hung up on your price tag in a totally different job market in which you did not succeed could be a dreadful error. "Does this mean giving up a better income for the rest of my life?" you ask. Not necessarily. Given the right environment, your chances of moving up the ladder are a lot better than if you persist in pursuing a career in the wrong one. As such, a lower price tag now could mean a high price tag later if you can relocate to a job universe in which your real value is better recognized by bosses and mentors.

NOW IT'S MY TURN!

1. Does your present position use all your skills?

2. If it doesn't, have you tried to find out whether there are any job universes that might?

3. In your present position, do you draw upon your past job experience as well as your skills?

4. Can you think of any different departments in your company that might call upon this previous experience as well as your talent? What options outside your company might use your previous experience as well as your skills?

5. In the job you have now, do you call upon your formal training as well as your past experience?

6. Can you think of any job opportunity within your company that might better capitalize on your training as well as your experience? Outside your company?

7. Are you using your nonwork skills or knowledge in your present employment?

8. Have you ever tried to find a position in which you used these nonwork skills or talents as well as your job knowledge?

9. If you have experience in only one department, have you thought about switching departments to secure a second kind of experience, which, when combined with the first, might give you a competitive edge later in your career?

10. Do you make personal marketing a daily event? Why not?

11. Do you pursue a continuing program to update your skills base so that you can offer more benefits to bosses and mentors?

12. Have you switched jobs relatively rapidly thus far in your career? Did you allow sufficient time in each position you held?

13. Have you held any positions too long? Thinking back to such a position, did this overly long tenure in one position affect the way you were perceived by higher-level people in your organization?

14. Had you made personal marketing a daily task, what could you have done to secure a promotion sooner? Did you try to increase your benefits base while you held that job? Did you pursue an awareness campaign? Did you make a conscious effort to develop a better image?

15. Do you keep an eagle eye out for changes in your organization that could in time create opportunities for you? Have you talked these opportunities over with your boss or mentors? Why?

16. Have you ever turned down an opportunity that intrigued you because the organization was not prepared to pay you more than the one you were in? Was it money alone that prompted your decision? Or was it partially pride?

17. Do you think that today you might have been more satisfied with the opportunity you let go by than with your present position?

18. Could you increase your income potential by trying to secure a position similar to your own in a larger company? Have you made an effort to create awareness of you with people in larger organizations? Why?

19. If you have moved from one part of the country to another in switching jobs, did you research cost-of-living differentials? Did you increase your purchasing power with such moves? Why?

chapter eleven

Developing a personal marketing plan that works!

July and August are wonderful months for most people: a time for vacations, trips to the beach, and so on. For brand managers, however, these two months are usually the toughest 61 days of the year. That's because during this period brand managers spend long evenings and lost weekends at the office researching and writing the first draft of their next year's marketing plan. This physical and mental endurance test doesn't end in August either. Once the plans have been drafted, they are submitted (often verbally as well as in writing) to the next level of company management, which invariably makes suggestions for changes that more often than not mean more hours of midnight toiling prior to the plan being presented again at the next highest organization level, and so on. Often these marketing plans go through three and four writings before top management signs off on the plan and it is implemented in January of the following year.

As you may have guessed by now, this book recommends that you write a personal marketing plan for yourself—one patterned after the plans brand managers write. Your first reaction to this idea may well be, "No, thank you! I'll skip that! After all, if brand plans are enough to spoil a brand manager's summer, why should a plan spoil mine?" If you do feel this way, keep these points in mind:

• A personal marketing plan can be an extremely useful tool in your pursuit of success in life, because it forces you to formally recognize where you now are in your career and where you want to take it in the next year and the next five years. Writing a plan makes your goals and actions to achieve these goals official. They become your benchmark to see if, by the end of the year, you have, in fact, achieved what you set out to do or if you have accomplished more or less than you hoped you might. It's a bogie that counts. If you just think through your plan (and don't put it down in black and white), it loses the tangibility that can goad you to achieve your goal and that can provide you with great satisfaction when you meet or exceed your written expectations.

• The second reason it pays to create an official personal marketing plan for yourself is that writing one is a heck of a lot easier than writing a brand plan. You don't need to submit it to anyone, therefore, it doesn't have to be letter-perfect or, for that matter, even typed. Your spelling doesn't count, and you don't need to burn the midnight oil calculating trends in sales, distribution, and so on. You are the person it is written for. Now, you might like to share your goals and action plans with your spouse, if you like, since he or she is probably going to have to be involved in both to a degree. And it would also pay for you to show the first draft to a close business associate to see if he or she agrees with achievability of your one- and five-year goals and the practicality of the plans you have made in order to achieve them. But nothing's official and ultimately you're the person who signs off on your own future.

• The best reason of all to write a personal marketing plan is that you have already done the hardest work required to turn one out. By answering the questions at the end of the previous ten chapters, you have done just about all the research you'll need to do. So it's just a matter of putting it all together. And it won't take that long to do. Carrying out your plan is what will take the real effort.

At this point, you may be coming around to the idea of writing a personal marketing plan, but you are reserving final judgment until you learn a little bit more about exactly what such a plan would be like. Fair enough. Let's consider a typical outline.

I. BACKGROUND TO YOUR PLAN

A. Your Track Record Versus the Track Record of Your Peers

1. The number of promotions you have had since you left school compared to the number of promotions that peers have had since they entered the same field.
2. Your trend in promotions. Have they been occurring more or less frequently in recent years, or do they happen like clockwork?
3. Initiation of promotions. Have your promotions come as a result of your prodding, or have they been thrust upon you by bosses or mentors?
4. Changes in organizations. If you have had to switch companies in order to secure better positions, try to explain why this was the case. Why weren't you promoted within the companies that you left?
5. Your assessment (based on paragraphs A1 through A4) of your chances for promotions in your present position if you do nothing at this point to improve your competitive-position.

B. Your Image Versus Your Peers' Image

1. The key elements of your present image as revealed by analyzing the factors outlined in Chapter 5.
2. An objective comparison of your shelf image against your perception of the images of peers in your immediate organization and peers in other related organizations who could potentially vie for promotion with you in future years. Pay particular attention in your evaluation to newcomers to your organization in the past year who are being evaluated for the first time. Ask yourself what was your initial impression rather than with-time impression. Also look critically for demonstrated changes in images of old timers who may have active image-changing programs of their own in progress.

C. Your Credentials (Back Label) Versus Your Peers'

1. A brief summary of the elements of your training, experience, natural talent, and associations that you believe have had an

impact on the buyers of you in the past and are part of your known credentials. Chapter 4 outlines the factors you should consider.

2. An objective comparison of your credentials against your perception of the credentials of peers in your immediate organization as well as potential peers who are at your level in other related organizations who might at some future date compete with you in your success market. As in B-2, pay particular attention to both newcomers being judged for the first time by your boss, potential bosses, and mentors and for those who have added to credentials since you evaluated them a year ago.

D. Your Benefits Capability Versus Your Peers'

1. The corporate benefits that you have delivered since securing your most recent position, with emphasis on those benefits that you delivered in the past year or two. Be as specific as possible in citing examples of tangible, meaningful benefits that you believe are associated with you. Quantify results as much as possible (e.g., few remember successful projects; many can remember the person who managed to find a shortcut which resulted in completing a project in 8 weeks rather than the planned 12).

As you consider the benefits you have delivered, make sure that you really own them. If bosses, peers, or mentors have assumed the glory that you believe you personally delivered, do not include these benefit examples in your appraisal of your own performance. Chances are they should be discussed in D-2 following.

As you analyze the corporate benefits you have delivered, put them into one of the four categories of corporate benefits described in Chapter 6. If you have provided benefits in only one, two, or three of the four categories, note this. It could be significant.

2. A brief comparison of the corporate benefits you delivered in the past (and particularly this past year) with those of the benefits ascribed to your immediate and potential peers with

whom you are familiar. In this short review of tangible corporate benefits delivered by your competition, try to assess the impact of their corporate contributions versus your own on the next several levels of your organization.

3. A brief summary of the personal benefits you have attempted to deliver to your boss, potential bosses, and mentors, with particular emphasis on those for which you have received obvious recognition. If you can, categorize the type of personal benefit you believe you have delivered and evaluate how many of the seven personal benefits you have consistently delivered in the past year.

4. A brief comparison of the personal benefits you and your competition have delivered to bosses, potential bosses, and potential peers, particularly during this past year. In making this comparison, try to assess the impact of the personal benefits that you and your competition delivered to key persons on the next several levels of your company.

E. Markets for Your Talents

1. Potential job universes. This is the place to identify *all* success markets in which you might compete were you to leave your present company or position. Even if you have absolutely no intention of leaving your present company, it might pay for you to include this section in your plan. That's because it will force you to at least consider what other industry and functional areas you might possibly pursue at this stage of your career were you to decide for one reason or another to switch companies or careers. (You'll find Chapter 3 can be helpful in suggesting ways to determine where you might pursue alternate pathways to the top should you have difficulty in developing a list.)

   Once you have developed your alternate success market list, rank all possibilities in terms of *your interest* in them. You might consider it convenient to make a summary table to indicate the possibilities and reason for ranking, such as the one shown below that might have been created by a line manufacturing person with computer hardware background.

FACTORS AFFECTING INTEREST

Potential Job Universes	Current size	Current profit	Growth rate
Personal computer	$ 000	00 %	00 %
Office computer	$ 000	00%	00%
Medical equipment using computer	$ 000	00%	00%
Communications equipment using computer	$ 000	00%	00%
Etc.	$ 000	00%	00%

2. Potential positions universes. You might also want to chart alternate functional areas in which your experience, training, and skills might qualify you for, indicating those factors that would affect your interest in pursuing them. The example shown below, which might have been developed by a person with a sales background, suggests a possible format for a position universes chart.

FACTORS AFFECTING INTEREST

Potential Positions	Current potential salaries	Growth Oppor.	Knowledge to be gained	Interest in job content
Line Sales Mgmt.	$35-50	very high	above average	high
Sales Trainer	$30-35	limited	limited	average
Sales Admin. Staff	$30-40	very low	average	low
Jr. Marketing pos.	$35-40	very high	high	very high
Sales Promotion pos.	$30-35	high	above average	very high

3. Success ranking. After you have charted alternate job and position universes, you should include a brief review of what you believe your probability of success might be in each area, without concern for your degree of interest in it. Again, for clarity, you might want to develop a table showing the alternatives and the factors that you consider to have an impact on

your success probability (e.g., technical knowledge or technical skills, managerial skills, communication skills, etc.). Here, you might want to rank the importance of each factor to each universe and your assessment of your ability in each area.

F. Buying Preferences of Your Boss, Potential Bosses, and Mentors

1. Briefly evaluate your competitive position in your organization based on how much you and your peers share in common with your boss. You'll find questions 2 through 6 at the end of Chapter 7 particularly helpful in assessing common associations, physical characteristics, personality, and performance that you and your peers share with key persons in your organization. If you feel so inclined, you might want to chart these common associations. If you do, the following example could prove to be of help to you:

IMMEDIATE AND POTENTIAL PEERS

Points in Common with Boss:

	YOU	Judy B.	Bryan A.	Kent P.	Michael J.	Sharon M.	Doug A.	Todd T.
schools attended:	Y				Y			
prior business affiliations		Y	Y					
certifications	Y		Y			Y	Y	
physical similarities					Y			Y
personalities	Y			Y	Y			
etc.								

2. A brief review of the backgrounds (credentials, experience, demographics) and physical and psychographic profiles of

those people who have been successful in your company, particularly in the recent past. You may also find it convenient to chart this analysis. It would look similar to the chart above— with matrices labeled "Successful People in Your Organization" and "Points in Common with One Another."

G. Awareness of You Versus Peers by Key People

1. A summary of the names and titles of potential mentors or bosses both within your company and within your industry who are personally aware of you as a result of business and nonbusiness associations. In developing this summary, give particular emphasis to those people who have become aware of you during the past year (or since you wrote your last personal marketing plan).

2. Your objective assessment of the quality and frequency of your contacts with potential mentors and bosses. If you have been able to provide personal benefits to any members of this awareness group, be sure to note this. You may find it convenient to summarize the group of potential bosses and mentors in table form such as the following, rather than to describe these people in a paragraph format. That's fine. (Remember this plan is written for you and no one need approve of its format).

POTENTIAL BOSS AND MENTOR AWARENESS

Name	Company or Department	# contacts in past year	Quality of Contacts	Sampled Personal Benefits
J. Jones	Strat. Plng.	2	VG	Y-Referral
B. Smith	Fin. Plng.	12	F (Co. Mtg.)	N
R. White	Intl. Foods	1	E. (on same indus. panel)	Y
etc.				

Total key people aware of you: 9
Total key people met in past year: 3
Total # of contacts with key people: 51

H. Other Factors Affecting Your Marketability

1. If you are planning a shift in your marketing strategy that involves a move from your present job, present company and/or present industry, include a brief, objective statement of the positioning advantages that might accrue to you in image or credentials as a result of your decision to pursue career development in a different success market that would benefit from your particular blend of prior experience. In this short description, be sure to note any disadvantages that could accrue as a result of this shift in marketplace (lowered awareness, lessened creditability, and so on).

2. If you are planning a shift in marketing yourself from within your present organization to another one inside your industry or in another industry, include a brief, objective summary of your pricing situation versus the marketplace in which you will compete. This review should be based on research, *not* opinion. If you are priced significantly above or below the going market rate for persons within the new marketplace in which you will compete, this could be a disadvantage. If your price tag is significantly higher, you will obviously secure fewer buyers unless you provide significantly more benefits than peers; if your price tag is significantly less, it may well impact on buyers' faith in the benefits that you offer to them.

3. If you are planning a campaign to secure a new position within your company or with another firm, include a brief objective review of any timing factors that could have an impact on your campaign. If you have been in your present position longer than your peers or longer than you were in your previous positions, for example, this could affect buyer acceptance. If, alternately, you have been in your present position less time than peers, it could have an impact on actual or perceived capability to deliver desired corporate benefits. It could also have an impact on previously started self-development programs that may not have been completed, so note these factors.

   If you are planning a campaign to secure a new position within or outside of your present company and are conducting this campaign against a finite timetable as a result of decision by your present boss (mutual or otherwise) that you must leave your present position, this timing situation should be addressed here.

If you are conducting a short-term campaign to secure another position, it is recommended that you follow the traditional job search strategies outlined in *How to Get a Better Job Quicker* or other, similar texts. It is, nonetheless, to your advantage to create a personal marketing plan using this outline to make sure your long-term strategy is consistent with your short-term job search goal.

I. Recent Developments Affecting Your Marketability

1. If you are in the process of enhancing your benefits capability or image through a self-development program that is not yet completed, include a reference to this here. If this is your situation, it would pay to address the issue of timing in your plan (F-3 above) since it could pay for you to complete your product-improvement effort prior to initiating any significant personal campaign.

2. If you have had a recent change in bosses but continue in the same position as before this change, you may wish to appraise as objectively as possible any recent shifts in your perceived benefits capability or image. This section can be particularly valuable if your previous boss was recently promoted to a higher level in your organization, and you were not promoted into your previous boss's position. Did a peer-competitor receive the promotion you expected? Was an outsider from another department or company awarded your boss's job? In either event, a significant shift in your perceived image and benefits capability may have taken place as a result, and you need to objectively appraise this recent development.

II. OVERALL PERSONAL GOALS AND OBJECTIVES

This is likely to be shortest section of your plan although it is perhaps the most important. The two subsections that comprise this section may be only a few paragraphs each.

A. Your One-Year Personal Goal and Strategy

Here you'll outline where you hope to be in 12 months time, and in broad brushstrokes, your primary strategy for achieving this goal. If you're wondering how to get started on this paragraph, you might say to yourself, "This time next year I would like to be . . ." and follow this thought with what you want and think you can realistically achieve in this timeframe. The examples shown below suggest the kinds of one-year goals you might set for yourself:

- "very close to promotion in my department."
- "considered as a serious candidate for a lateral move to the ____(name)____ group."
- "out of the training program and into a full-time line assignment."
- "in a supervisory position, and no longer an individual contributor."
- "in a similar position in another company in my industry. (I believe my present company will always view me as a blue-collar worker even though I completed college at night, and I need to begin in a new company with a college grad image.)"
- "in a similar position to the one I'm now in but in the software programming industry. (I believe my skills are appropriate in this field, and that I have a better chance for long-term growth than as a program analyst where I am now working in the car manufacturing industry.)"

Follow up your goal statement with a short summary of the overall strategy you plan to use to attain your goal. The examples following suggest the kinds of strategy statements you might make. You'll note that they don't go into detail. (Your specific plans will; they are addressed later.)

- "Continue the image-correction program I began two years ago to counter the impulsive image I had gained prior to that time. (Image correction needed for desired promotion.)"
- "Conduct an aggressive leadership sampling campaign aimed at section leaders in sister departments who could

be sources of promotion to group level for me during
the next year."

- "Intensify personal benefits campaign aimed at my
boss's boss."
- "Begin awareness and sampling program aimed at alumni
peers and superiors in the division I recently joined to
better understand opportunities for growth that could
be pursued."
- "Conduct a traditional job search to secure a position in
the advertising industry as an account executive in next
six months. (I believe my sales background plus degree
in communications makes this possible.)"
- "Begin awareness campaign among ad agency account
supervisors in second six months." (Changing companies
or industries does not obviate the need for full-year goals
and strategies.)

You may find in developing your one-year goal and strategy section that you have several parallel goals. Fine! If you do, be sure
to indicate them in their order of priority, and be sure, too, that
these goals are consistent with one another. You may also determine that you should undertake a multiple-pronged strategy in
order to achieve a single goal or consistent multiple goals. This is
most reasonable on your part since it is likely in some instances
that no single strategy would insure you of achieving your goal.
If you do elect to indicate several strategies in this section, be
sure to put a priority on each. And make sure in writing this section that you are dealing in broad-brush strategies, not specific
programs. (These we'll come to later in your plan outline.)

B. Your Five-Year Personal Goal and Strategy

In this section you'll outline where you hope to be in five years'
time, assuming that you are successful in achieving your one-year
goal on or near schedule. As you think about your five-year goal,
keep in mind that the goal you achieve *this* year will serve as a
springboard for future progress. As such, a host of questions
about your future options may come to mind. For example:

- If you gain a new credential in a year's time, will this
permit you to explore alternate job universes or func-

tional opportunities that you weren't even able to consider as you write your current personal marketing plan?

- If you have significantly improved your capacity to deliver meaningful corporate benefits within your own organization as a result of a people-skills self-development program you have undertaken and completed by this time next year, would you be better off pursuing growth within your own organization or marketing your talents to other organizations in your field or outside of it?

- If the awareness campaign you undertake this year pays off and you are known by several highly-placed persons in different departments within your company, which direction should you pursue?

Keep in mind, too, that you might not achieve your one-year goal on schedule. This, too, would affect your five-year goal possibilities. As such, it would pay for you to develop the most reasonable and achievable one-year goal and to consider several reasonable and achievable five-year goals that follow logically from it. Obviously, you'll have a preference priority for each of these five-year possibilities, but at the same time, it stands to reason that your five-year goal is subject to a good many variables beyond your control! (You can understand why career planning beyond the five-year forecast really doesn't make much sense and why a five-year strategy statement is not even included in this marketing plan outline).

III. SPECIFIC PLANS FOR THE COMING YEAR

This section of the plan will be ten pages long! This doesn't mean you have to write ten pages, only that it covers ten topics and it's probably a good idea to devote a separate page in your plan to each of them. Each of these topics represents a specific action category that could affect your progress towards your one-year goal. Not surprisingly, each category is featured in this book so that at this point you should have a pretty good idea of how this category might apply to your own situation. As you consider each of these action categories, you might come to the conclusion that one or more of them wouldn't have an impact on your one-year goal and so isn't worth including in your plan. Quite possibly this is the case. Nonetheless, by including a sepa-

3. *Review components for possible assembly savings.* (Check out 200 components to see if some could be subassembled by vendors to avoid production bottlenecks.)
4. *Any projects you might want to look into in the next 12 months.* (Even blue sky projects that you believe could have a significant corporate benefits payoff deserve to be included in your outline.)

B. Personal Benefits Delivery

On this action category page, you list specific projects you have already undertaken or plan to begin and/or complete in the next 12 months that will deliver benefits of personal value to bosses and mentors. If you were in accounting, for example, you might come up with projects like these:

1. *Work on ideas to make it easier for the boss to check my reconciliations.* Marking headings in different colors? Stapling machine tabs to spread sheets? Using my home computer to make printout for items we haven't put on office computer yet? Any of these simple ideas could make the boss's life easier and that is my primary goal.
2. *Support the campaign of my boss's boss to bring cost and product accounting sections under his control.* It's obvious that my boss' boss thinks the current organizational setup subverts his authority. I could let him know of examples that he could use to sell management on consolidating departments under his control. This support will demonstrate my personal loyalty which is my secondary goal.
3. Any specific ideas or plans you have for delivery of one or more of the seven basic human needs outlined in Chapter 6 belong on this action category page.

If you feel the need to fill several pages with ideas in any one action category, do so! There's no restriction on length of your plan whatsoever. Do keep in mind that you don't need to spell out each of your projects in the detail shown here. The paragraphs shown here are illustrative only. If you can communicate to yourself the specific projects you plan to undertake in any action category in a single sentence, great! Remember, the plan is to help you organize your efforts to sell yourself better. Do whatever it takes to do this. But be sure to write down something. Projects planned in your head are unlikely to get accomplished.

C. Self-Improvement Program—Package

On this action category page, jot down the projects and programs you have begun which you will begin, and/or which you will complete in the next 12 months to create a more favorable image for yourself. Your list may run from mundane to esoteric and could include:

1. Get a new blue-pinstriped suit for meetings with the boss's boss to project a more conservative image.
2. Start playing handball again to get rid of that excess 20 pounds I've been carrying and to make me look trimmer, more concerned about my appearance.
3. Buy one of those executive organizer systems I've been meaning to buy so that the boss won't catch me overlooking any project, no matter how small, as he has in the past (and which subverts my desired image of thoroughness).
4. Include in this section all the things you are doing or could do to upgrade your image and exactly what way you expect your project to enhance your image. (Have a precise purpose in mind.) If some projects cost money, put a priority on them and do the ones now that you think rank high. Maybe you'll carry forward some of your projects to your next year's plan. So be it. No one says you have to complete every project you plan for yourself within 12 months of your plan date. But there's a much greater chance you'll complete some if you take the time to jot them down and cross them off as you finish them.

D. Self-Improvement Program—Back Label

On this action category page, indicate the self-improvement programs that you are currently participating in or that you plan to begin or complete with the next 12 months. In developing your list, be sure you cite the specific objective you hope to achieve by participating in each program on your list. The number of programs you propose for yourself isn't important. The duration of each program isn't important. The place you are taking the program isn't important unless, of course, your objective is to have completed a program at a prestigious institution. What is important is how your back label (credentials) will be upgraded when you have completed the program you are in or intend to enroll in during the 12 months. Ask yourself who will be impressed by your credential and why.

Remember, too, that some credentials could be meaningless in pursuit of the success market in which you are competing. To enroll in self-development programs just for the sake of enrolling is pointless. You may well be better off in working harder on self-development programs with no impact on your back label, but that could help you deliver corporate or personal benefits more effectively. These are, of course, the subject of the next action category page of your plan. Consult Chapter 8 for an array of potential back label-enhancing programs you might consider, and if there are several that seem appropriate, put a priority on each.

If you elect not to pursue any, note the reason why on this page. This reason why could reflect personal considerations (time, location, and the like). Your reason for not pursuing any self-development programs may be because you think there is no gain to be achieved within your present organization or other organizations. So be it. But be sure to jot your reasons down, so that you are absolutely sure it doesn't pay to continue developing yourself in some way.

E. Self-Development Programs—Corporate Benefits Delivery

On this action category page, list the programs or courses you intend to pursue not for the credentials that they provide you, but for the manner in which they increase your capacity to deliver corporate benefits. In developing your list, be sure to keep in mind any technological trends in your business. By planning each year to keep up with knowledge necessary to maintain existing benefits delivery capacity, you can avoid becoming technically obsolescent by oversight.

Your list could include programs that would not enable you to provide more or better corporate benefits for your present organization. If this is the case, however, you should have a purpose in mind in developing skills or knowledge that are nonwork-related. If these skills will enable you to provide corporate benefits to other companies or in other job universes that you might pursue in future years, jot this fact down. The point is to assure yourself that any investment you make of either time or money in improving your ability to deliver benefits will have a payoff to you in some way at some time. Developing new skills just for the sake of developing new skills is fine if it is your goal to become a renaissance person. But admit this to yourself before you start. You may well decide that enhancing your skills repertoire in a way that could increase your corporate benefits delivery makes more sense since it is likely to propel you ahead in whatever success market you pursue.

F. Self-Improvement Program—Personal Benefits Delivery

On this action category page, jot down anything you are doing or plan to do to improve your capacity to deliver personal benefits by this time next year. Your list could include doing nothing more than reading books on motivation (state the titles in your plan; be specific!). Or, it could involve courses or seeing a psychologist or counsellor (state the names of the courses and the reasons you selected them; state your purpose in pursuing each element of your personal benefits-upgrading program).

If you need ideas for pursuing such programs, see Chapter 8. And if you don't elect to continue developing your ability to deliver personal benefits, jot this down, too. It is the author's view that programs in this category are perhaps the best investment of your time and money in pursuing all the success that is in you. More people fail to make it as far as they might because of a weakness in this area than in any other. Plan on at least one project a year in this category. You won't regret it.

G. Awareness Development and/or Maintenance Programs

On this action category page, you'll note the following:
1. What kinds of people you want to get to meet in the next 12 months, both within your present organization and outside of it. State titles, types of organizations, and why you consider

it important to meet them on this page. The more specific you are, the better.

2. Who you'd like to meet if you already know of people you feel you should get to know in order to create paths for advancement either this year or in following years. If there are a number of people, put a priority on each so you can direct your efforts accordingly.

3. Your action programs you intend to pursue in order to meet the kinds of people cited in G1 or the specific individuals cited in G2. If you intend to pursue a variety of programs, put a priority on those that you believe will allow you to meet the most people, have the most contact with those people whom you believe are of greatest potential benefit to your career, or provide you with opportunities for quality contacts (those providing opportunities to sample your corporate or personal benefits).

4. Your action programs that you are now pursuing or intend to pursue in order to maintain ongoing relationships with those people you do meet who you believe are in a position to advance your career.

H. Positioning Plan and Program

This action category page should be incorporated into your plan regardless of whether you are contemplating leaving your organization for another industry or not. This page should review:

1. Your action program to uniquely position yourself in your present position based on more effective utilization of different past experiences, training, and/or skills development combined together to enable you to actually provide better corporate or personal benefits or to create a more positive image of you in your present organization. As an example, if you are a marketing manager who has not used previously developed creative-writing skills (say, learned in school), your action program might be to write your own promotional materials in the coming 12 months rather than turn this task over to an advertising agency or another department. This would enable you to save your company money (a corporate benefit)

based on positioning yourself as a marketing manager with a unique communications ability.

2. Your action program to develop future positioning opportunities within the next five years. This would involve initiating a program within the next 12 months to undertake additional training or skills development programs, to shift to another functional position in your own company, to seek out a new affiliation in another company, or to provide you with an opportunity to combine your current and planned experience at a later date to provide you with unique positioning advantage within the next five years. As an example, you might now be an accounting supervisor and have as your Action Program for the next 12 months "to seek a transfer as a supervisor to the systems department," with your five-year plan to include the capability of positioning yourself as the financial systems expert in your company.

I. Pricing

This section of your plan should include:

1. Any action programs you plan to undertake in order to secure a position in a better-paying industry. This could involve a traditional job search campaign during the coming 12 months or a longer-term plan to meet and sample yourself to persons within the industry you have selected.
2. Any action programs you plan in order to secure a position with another company or within your own company at a location in a part of the country where compensation levels are constant, but purchasing power is greater.
3. A recap of any action programs you plan in order to prepare yourself for a higher-paying position within your own company or industry. This could be simply a reference to a positioning program you are undertaking, to promotions or offers you hope to achieve as a result of an intensive benefits delivery campaign during the coming year, or to an image-enhancement program that you are about to undertake.

J. Timing

This section of your plan should include:

1. Any specific timing factors that have an impact on the start or

completion date of any action programs described elsewhere in your plan.

2. A spread sheet showing the start and completion date of all action programs incorporated into your plan. This monthly timetable need not be a work of art. The purpose of this spread sheet is to provide you with visual control of your action programs. By penciling in the start date of each program, the duration of each, and any heavy workload periods you anticipate with each action program, you'll be able to avoid overworking yourself at any point in time, and where there is a sequence required to any action programs you plan, to avoid starting one prior to the completion of another, related effort. Your timetable could look something like this:

PERSONAL MARKETING PLAN —
1984 SPREAD SHEET

Action Category** & Project Title	Jan	Feb	Mar	Apr	and so on
A. Corporate Benf'ts Act'n Proj't #1*	heavy workload				
A.P. #2*			-----------------		
A.P. #3*				-----------------	
B. Personal Benf'ts A.P. #1*		---			
A.P. #2*			heavy workload		
C. Package Develm't A.P. #1*	--------				
A.P. #2*		-------------------			
D. Etc.					

*If you give each action project a number on each action category page, you won't need to write in the project title. (If you don't number projects, use titles.)

**Your spread sheet should include action programs from all action categories in your personal marketing plan.

IV. APPENDIX TO YOUR PERSONAL MARKETING PLAN

If you have amassed any documents that have influenced your plan, you might want to incorporate them into the appendix to your plan for future reference. Here you might add xerographic copies of:

- Performance evaluations by bosses suggesting strengths and weaknesses and areas for personal growth.

- articles about successful people in your field who you are trying to emulate in style or career path.
- a chart of your career progress to date showing when promotions occurred and time between promotions.
- scores on testing devices you have utilized in the past and which have profiled for you abilities and personality strengths and weaknesses.
- compensation studies of persons with your training and background indicating differences between industries and parts of the country. These studies could have been the basis for your decision to implement action programs leading towards better compensation for your efforts.
- And so on.

IS IT WORTHWHILE TO DEVELOP A PERSONAL MARKETING PLAN?

After reviewing the elements of your personal marketing plan outline, you may come to the conclusion that it might take a little more effort on your part to write your plan than you thought it might—even if you already answered the questions included at the end of each chapter of this book. There is no question that you can't hope to knock off your first personal marketing plan in a couple of hours. It may well take a day. Or a weekend. Even two weekends. Fortunately, once you have written your first personal marketing plan, you'll find it takes a good deal less time to write a second plan a year from now. (That's because you'll only need to add in a year's worth of information to the background section of your plan. You'll follow this year's format next year, so you won't be starting from scratch.)

The real hurdle facing you now is to make the decision to write your first personal marketing plan. You may be asking yourself even at this late stage of this book if it is all worth the effort in your particular instance. In answering this question for yourself, keep in mind that the moment you complete your plan (whether it be hastily put together or methodically written and revised), you are likely to put yourself ahead of ten thousand other persons with whom you compete in your success market. Only you will have:

1. Catalogued the factors that bear upon your course of action in the next year.

2. Set yourself an overall goal in writing of where you want to be in a year's time. (The keys to attainment of any goal are its precise definition and its tangibility.)

3. Thought out a series of action programs (small and/or large) that you intend to undertake during the next 12 months in order to meet your goals.

4. Given yourself tangible benchmarks against which you can judge your progress and a basis for establishing next year's goals.

Given the power to set yourself apart that a personal marketing plan provides you, you may well decide to give it a try, and you won't regret it! But even if you put off writing a plan for yourself, this book should give your career a lift. Perhaps it won't put you ahead of ten thousand other people, but knowing and practicing the seven principles of personal marketing success should give you the advantage in securing for yourself the most you can hope to achieve in your career. And so, as you approach the close of this book, here is one final suggestion:

> Don't put this book away forever. Plan to read Chapter 2 at least once a year—perhaps on the anniversary of your joining your present organization. And take an extra moment or two to reanswer the questions at the end of Chapters 1 through 10. As you change and grow each year, so will your answers to these questions change, and they will suggest to you new approaches for marketing your talents.

If you do this, there should be no doubt in your mind: *You will achieve your full potential in your quest for success!*

Index